Leo

24 July – 23 August

*First published in Great Britain 2008
by Harlequin Mills & Boon Limited,
Eton House, 18-24 Paradise Road, Richmond, Surrey TW9 1SR*

Copyright © Dadhichi Toth 2007, 2008 & 2009

ISBN: 978 0 263 86908 8

Typeset at Midland Typesetters Australia

*Harlequin Mills & Boon policy is to use papers that are
natural, renewable and recyclable products and made from
wood grown in sustainable forests. The logging and
manufacturing processes conform to the legal environmental
regulations of the country of origin.*

*Printed and bound in Spain
by Litografia Rosés S.A., Barcelona*

About
Dadhichi

Dadhichi is one of Australia's foremost astrologers, and is frequently seen on TV and in the media. He has the unique ability to draw from complex astrological theory to provide clear, easily understandable advice and insights for people who want to know what their future may hold.

In the 25 years that Dadhichi has been practising astrology, and conducting face and other esoteric readings, he has provided over 9,000 consultations. His clients include celebrities, political and diplomatic figures and media and corporate identities from all over the world.

Dadhichi's unique blend of astrology and face reading helps people fulfil their true potential. His extensive experience practising western astrology is complemented by his research into the theory and practice of eastern forms of astrology.

Dadhichi has been a guest on many Australian television shows and several of his political and worldwide forecasts have proved uncannily accurate. He has appeared on many of Australia's leading television networks and is a regular columnist for several Australian magazines.

His websites www.astrology.com.au, www.facereader.com and soulmate.com.au which attract hundreds of thousands of visitors each month, offer a wide variety of features, helpful information and services.

❦

Dedicated to The Light of Intuition
Sri V. Krishnaswamy — mentor and friend

With thanks to Julie, Joram, Isaac and Janelle

❦

Welcome from
Dadhichi

Dear Friend,

It's a pleasure knowing you're reading this, your astrological forecast for 2009. There's nothing more exciting than looking forward to a bright new year and considering what the stars have in store and how you might make the most of what's on offer in your life.

Apart from the anticipation of what I might predict will happen to you, of what I say about your upcoming luck and good fortune, remember that astrology is first and foremost a tool of personal growth, self-awareness and inner transformation. What 'happens to us' is truly a reflection of what we're giving out; the signals we are transmitting to our world, our universe.

The astrological adage of 'As above, so below' can also be interpreted in a slightly different way when I say 'As within, so without'! In other words, as hard as it is to believe, the world and our experiences of it, or our relationships and circumstances, good or bad, do tend to mirror our own belief systems and mental patterns.

It is for this reason that I thought I'd write a brief introductory note to remind you that the stars are pointers to your wonderful destiny and that you must work with them to realise your highest and most noble goals. The greatest marvel and secret is your own inner self! Astrology reveals these inner secrets of your character, which are the foundation of your life's true purpose.

What is about to happen to you this year is exciting, but what you *do* with this special power of knowledge, how you share your talents with others, and the way you truly enjoy each moment of your life is far more important than knowing *what* will happen. This is the key to a 'superior' kind of happiness. It will start to open up to you when you live in harmony with your true nature as shown by astrology.

I really hope you enjoy your coming twelve months, and gain new insights and fresh perspectives on your life through studying your 2009 horoscope. Here's hoping great success will be yours and health, love and happiness will follow wherever you go.

I leave you now with the words of a wise man, who once said:

Sow a thought, and you reap an act;
Sow an act, and you reap a habit;
Sow a habit, and you reap a character;
Sow a character, and you reap a destiny.
Your thoughts are the architects of your destiny.

Warm regards, and may the stars shine brightly for you in 2009!

Your Astrologer,

Dadhichi Toth

Contents

The Leo Identity 9

Leo: A Snapshot 10

Star Sign Compatibility 27

2009: The Year Ahead 51

2009: Month By Month Predictions 61

January 62

February 66

March 70

April 74

May 78

June 82

July 86

August..90

September 94

October..98

November 102

December 106

2009: Astronumerology............................111

2009: Your daily planner 133

The Leo Identity

Inspiration and genius—one and the same.

—Victor Hugo

Leo: A Snapshot

Key Characteristics

Pioneering, commanding, inflexible, ambitious, loyal, physical, generous, regal

Compatible Star Signs

Aries, Sagittarius, Gemini, Libra

Key Life Phrase

I shine

Life Goals

To set an example to others and lead with integrity

Platinum Assets

Great strength, vitality and magnetism

Zodiac Totem

The Lion

Zodiac Symbol

♌

Zodiac Facts

Fifth sign of the zodiac; fixed, hot, masculine, dry

Element

Fire

Famous Leos

Andy Warhol, Beatrix Potter, Belinda Carlisle, Billy Bob Thornton, Charlize Theron, Edward Norton, Eric Bana, Geri Halliwell, J.K. Rowling, Halle Berry, Hilary Swank, Kate Beckinsale, Napoleon Bonaparte, Pete Sampras, Jennifer Lopez, Sandra Bullock, Arnold Schwarzenegger, Ben Affleck, Madonna, Robert de Niro, Bill Clinton

Key to karma, spirituality and emotional balance

In your past life, Aries and its ruler Mars had a strong influence on you, which has led to your current zest for life. Your keywords are 'I shine' and therefore it's important not to let your desire for attention overpower your humility. Give selflessly of your time to others to grow spiritually yourself.

Jupiter rules Thursdays and is friendly to you. Learn to relax more and carry out your meditations on this day. This will accelerate your psychic insights. Take calming baths and use jasmine, sandalwood and orange to help connect you with your higher self.

Leo: Your profile

The centre of our solar system is the glowing Sun, which just so happens to be your ruler, Leo. Just like the bright and shining celestial Sun you too bring character, support and energy to our world.

In reflecting the characteristics of the Sun, you're full of dynamic energy. Few star signs have the same level of drive and self-motivation that you do. Your fire element is at the heart of this leonine energy and is recognisable in every aspect of your life—work, love and play.

You have a pioneering approach and love to be the first and best at everything you do. Because you exhibit so much self-confidence, you tend to outshine many of your peers who are usually quite prepared to let you take the lead because you do it so well with a sense of generosity and love.

Generosity is one key aspect of your Sun sign. Excuse me for referring to the Sun in so many instances, but it does reflect your personality so well. Warm and impartial in the way you shine your rays of love, you're happy to distribute what you have either materially or spiritually to anyone and everyone. Giving is a natural part of your nature.

You have a great mind and 'think big'. Your efforts are always sincere and unrelenting. Your sign is one of the fixed zodiac signs, which means you are determined and also at times a little inflexible if you set your mind and heart to something.

You are encouraging to others and like to see your friends and loved ones as successful as yourself, so you never refuse the help that is requested to get them to their goals as well.

You are so dramatic sometimes that some people might think you're a little over the top. But you don't care: because of your love of life and your high degree of optimism, you know that not everyone will accept you for who you are.

Arnold Schwarzenegger is a great example of the true Leo spirit. Successful in more than one line of activity, when you hear Arnold speak you can hear his sincerity and see his larger-than-life character coming through in everything he does. As you now know, Arnold has reached a high-level position being Governor of California.

You are dedicated and loyal to a fault. You are a genuine friend but expect the same in return from those with whom you wish to spend your time.

Conversely, you are a proud person and those who choose to tread their life path with you need to understand that the Leo ego can be severely wounded through any form of disloyalty or under-handedness. If you discover that someone has crossed you, you can be a formidable competitor and will win at any cost.

Humility is one of your lessons in life. You love praise and attention because this makes you feel as though your efforts have not been in vain. Success for Leo, however, is not a selfish action as the fruits of your labour are shared with those you love.

Many Leos reach the pinnacle of their professions due to their ambitious nature. Others recognise your unique abilities, even if they don't know you too well. You make a powerful impression everywhere you go.

You have a competitive spirit that draws you into sports and other games of chance. The totem of the lion is the king of the jungle, full of energy, drive and control. The physical appetites and level of energy are extraordinarily high and you will take great pleasure in directing these powerful forces into sports activities where you can excel and, if you choose, even pursue this line professionally (just like your totem).

You have an inflexible nature and this is sometimes seen as having an impervious path, demanding excellence from those who work and live with you. This is simply your way of making sure that others aspire to be their best. Unfortunately, you may sometimes be greatly misunderstood.

Three classes of Leo

You are a born leader and people feel protected under your guidance. This is particularly true if you are born in the first part of Leo; that is, between the 24th of July and the 2nd of August. You have an extra dose of solar energy as part of your makeup. You are very powerful, magnetic and attract good luck as part of your destiny. A public or high-profile position might be part of your life path.

If you were born between the 3rd and the 12th of August, your mind is always searching for excitement and adventure. You have a bold spirit and love to travel if you were born in the mid portion of Leo. Adventure and meeting people from all walks of life will fascinate you. You are quite a casual and easy-going person. In your relationships you may find it hard to settle down. You seek freedom in all areas of your life and this is the key to a satisfactory relationship.

As a Leo born between the 13th and 23rd of August, your energy is sometimes too erratic and impulsive. You need to become a little more conscious of others and their inability to keep up with you. You'll always work hard and have a generous heart. Don't forget to give yourself some time out to relax because you're always on the go. The spirit of competition is strong in you and you are out there to win.

Leo role model: Pete Sampras

Pete Sampras, the world famous tennis player, is born under Leo, just as you are. What a competitive and successful individual he has been! A great showman, but also dedicated to becoming a master of his craft, these traits perfectly reflect the true Leo spirit.

Leo: The light side

Your aura is palpable. In other words, people only have to walk into the same room as you to feel your dazzling presence. This is, as I have already mentioned, because of your connection to the solar disc, which is the ruler of Leo. You radiate sunshine and joy wherever you go

Leo has the ability to heal and uplift others, even unconsciously. Through your personality and warm gestures others feel happy and inspired by your actions. People look up to you and therefore Leo is one of the better role models of the zodiac in terms of what it is like to be an all-round good person.

People admire you as a leader, and in your social, professional and even family lives you take command and help steer people in the right direction. You are loyal in family life and make a great parent. You only have to look at the lioness with her cubs to see just how protective and nurturing she is.

Your intuition is very strong and you are able to couple this with a deep intuitive power as well. You can apply that to your commercial life where you have a knack of spotting a good deal and exercising your great sense of timing.

You are a born salesperson; therefore, your words contain great power to convince others of your position. You are persuasive and, even if people oppose you at first, it doesn't take long for you to bring them around to your way of thinking. Your enthusiasm is infectious and everyone you come in touch with will feel the joy that you do.

Leo: The shadow side

Your power is so strong that it is sometimes overwhelming. If you do become the boss or take on the leadership role (or rather should I say 'when'), you must be careful not to become overbearing in your manner. It is one thing to be respected, but another to be feared. Others may find your power just too much to handle.

If you set yourself a course of action, you have the tendency to go at it full-throttle and sometimes might not be reasonable enough to listen to the opinions or suggestions of others. This can be a mistake and cause you to alienate the very people who can become your best allies. Try to listen a little more and don't always assume that you are 100 per cent correct.

Your major life lessons centre on accepting that we are all equals. Yes, you are able to mix with all types of people, but your ego can sometimes get the better of you. Don't let the phrase 'Might makes right' dominate your relationships. Fortunately, Leo has the spiritual Sun as its ruler, which means that you are able to adopt a position of self-awareness and slowly but surely eradicate these character defects, which will bring you to a much more fulfilling position in life.

Leo woman

Grace and taste stand out as key words when describing women born under the sign of Leo. You also have the prowess of the lioness that is your ruling totem. Strength, grace, warmth and a natural protective instinct combine to reveal a complex but fascinating woman. And that you are!

You instinctively feel that you are destined to achieve important things in life. By this I don't necessarily mean fame in the traditional sense, but to do something that will make the world a better place and can give you a sense at the end of your life that you did make a difference.

You are a dignified, proud and independent person and, if others aren't prepared to help you achieve your goals, you are quite capable of treading the path alone.

Leo women have a tremendous amount of sex appeal and men are naturally attracted to them. It can be a deceptive game for the opposite sex, however, as men are surprised when they discover the strength and resilience of the female lion. You will need someone who can match these inherent powers of your character.

You enjoy the company of both women and men, and your honesty is often quite disarming. You know that in the modern world this is a rare commodity and you sometimes use this to great advantage. People don't quite know how to react to your straightforward and often blunt demands or responses. Your attitude is 'What you see is what you get'.

In your choice of friends, you need to know that integrity is paramount. This is a reflection of your own standards and ideals and anything less than this is unacceptable. Even if you were born into difficult social or economic circumstances, your sheer drive and willpower to better yourself wins out. You like to associate yourself with others who exhibit the same level of strength, the same level of inner fortitude and ambition. You expect people to whom you are close to be as powerful if not more powerful than you.

Some Leo women may find this high benchmark too difficult for others to meet and prefer to go it alone because they can't handle settling for second best. Just like many felines, the Leo woman is sometimes just as solitary.

Shopping is one of your favourite pastimes and this is where you can seek out those clothes that perfectly reflect your flamboyant and dramatic personality. Apart from that you love a good bargain and don't mind haggling to get the best deal. You always look your best and, even if you are out and about having a casual day, people are surprised to see how impeccably dressed and well presented you are.

Your self-esteem is high, but fortunately this works from the inside out and therefore what you have, as they say, shouldn't be 'what you base your sense of security on'.

You have a great love of children and the reason you get on so well with them is that you are able to step into their shoes and feel what it's like to be a kid again. Because of this you will stay young at heart, even into your old age.

Life to you is a journey of excitement, fun and adventure. You make a great friend and will give of yourself 100 per cent when called upon. The Leo woman is indeed in a special calibre of people.

Leo man

Power, strength and any other superlative word depicting vitality and leadership describe the male Leo personality to a 't'.

Due to the rulership of the Sun, which is a masculine 'planet', you perfectly reflect these qualities in your personality.

Because Leo is one of the most regal signs, representing the king of the jungle and the zodiac, most Leo males will never do anything that is beneath them. You hold your head up high even under the most adverse circumstances, so when I speak of strength, I talk of intestinal stamina and the power to overcome.

You are passionate, competitive and sometimes aggressive but always single-minded in your desire to obtain your goals. Some may call you inflexible, but I prefer to use the words relentless and persistent to describe your ability to win out, even against great odds. Your confidence is so strong that even those who are weak-willed and lacking in character seem to absorb your radiance and feel inspired to become better people.

Your courageous nature and bold, dramatic actions mean you can serve as a model for others and many have been benefited through the positive mental attitude of the Leo male. Some people perceive you as bombastic and may feel that you boast far too much about your achievements and what you wish to do, but actually they misunderstand your motivation for being like this.

Your ego is a harmless one to a large extent and these expressions are your way of sharing your enthusiasm with everyone around you. You want to engage them, make them part of your plans and share the spoils. Bad luck to those who can't see through your bright exterior to the softer more compassionate side of your nature.

You are a high-principled person, working hard to take the lead. You see the potential in others, often more than they can see it in themselves, and therefore push others to their limits. Unbeknown to them, this is not an act of cruelty, but your way of bringing out the best in them.

As a father you can be incredibly demanding and may even expect the impossible from your children. This again relates to what I have said in the last paragraph. Bear in mind, however, that people are not always able to get the gist of where you are coming from. Take things a little more slowly and others will appreciate who you are more readily.

Your protectiveness is another one of your great traits. If you decide to marry you can really show your love through the way you take care of your spouse and children. You are honourable and loyal and usually marry for life. Being generous to a fault, your loved ones will never go without.

For the Leo male I can safely predict you will achieve much in life because you have the strength and composure to gain success where others don't. Try to overcome the vanity trap and stay humble; stick to your plans and happiness as well as success will be yours.

Leo child

A bundle of warm, loving joy is what they are: I am talking about the child of Leo. Happy, vivacious and somewhat bois-terous as well as cheeky, you still forgive them these character flaws for the sheer delight that they will bring into your life.

Ruled by the warm and light-giving Sun, these children are born actors who like to play, frolic and at times challenge you with their dramatic antics.

Leo children are born leaders and are definitely the central figure in their peer groups, even from an early age. They are bold and courageous in what they do, so you do need to steer them onto the right course as early as possible.

Sometimes your little Leo is somewhat wilful and this is based upon their extremely high levels of self-confidence. The big-head-on-small-shoulders aspect of their nature is often a challenge for parents but, as I said, there is more than enough in their personalities to compensate for this.

Because young Leos are extremely competitive, sporting activities are essential to help them let off steam and to develop self-discipline and good life skills as well.

They are very vital and love such sports as football, basketball and swimming. Physical activities come naturally to them and don't be surprised if they choose to develop these skills to a competitive or even professional level later in their lives.

Your Leo child craves loving, affection and attention. By giving them the love that they yearn for, you will foster a deep and lifelong bond with them.

If you need to correct your child, make sure you do it constructively and not in a way that demeans them or humiliates them, particularly in front of their peers. This will affect them permanently.

Because the young lion needs space and is at times solitary, allow them their free time to do what they will. Make sure, however, that they get adequate sleep because lions and cats are also nocturnal.

Romance, love and marriage

Leo naturally rules the fifth sphere of the zodiac that relates to love affairs, creativity and future karma. Along with this, it has relevance to children and the relationships associated with them.

For this reason, love and romance seem to be particularly natural activities for you, Leo.

Being in love and sharing the emotional part of your nature is very, very important to you and will play a significant role in your future happiness. Along with this, entertainment and any sort of pleasure will be part and parcel of your romantic association. You need a social environment in which to show off your partner and communicate how you feel with your friends. Love is not a selfish thing to you. You want everyone to share in your joy.

In a social situation, you like to take the lead and rarely feel daunted, even in large crowds. Sometimes others who don't know you that well misunderstand you. A good piece of advice for you, especially if you're looking to develop new friendships with groups of people you don't know too well, is to go slowly and don't be too theatrical in your initial advances, otherwise they might misinterpret your motivation.

Because you are larger than life in almost everything you do, others are intimidated by you, particularly rivals who might possibly be vying for the same lover. This could invite opposition and fierce rivalry. Unfortunately for these people, they don't realise that you are up to the challenge of fighting for what you believe is yours.

You have ample opportunity to mix with people of all persuasions and to be selective in the type of partner you wish to have as a soulmate. You like the idea of being challenged and don't quite feel as if you deserve a love that hasn't been fought for.

Once you do become attached, your partner will learn that you are somewhat difficult to please; but, by the same token, you offer much in return. You are warm, affectionate and will serve your partner in every way possible.

Your loyalty is second to none and once you give your heart to someone there's no mistaking your true love. You expect your partner to be equally loyal and can be unforgiving if your trust at any stage is broken. You need to make this known at the outset of any relationship or friendship you enter into because you can quickly be decisive and this can be a crushing blow to someone who hasn't seen your wrath coming.

Sexuality is particularly important to you and, although this doesn't fall strictly under the same area as entertainment and love affairs, sex is a natural extension of your playful nature. Leo males are particularly sexual, but both of the sexes exude a type of animal magnetism that others find irresistible.

Because the marriage zone for Leo is the sign of Aquarius, relationships are not always settled until midlife. Saturn and Uranus have a hand to play in this and can indicate some false starts to fulfilment on an emotional level.

Once you settle for the right partner, you do so for life and will expect the relationship to be mutually fulfilling in every respect. You are prepared to put in the hard yards to make it a successful partnership. Your standards are very high and you are ardent and demonstrative.

You make a wonderful impression wherever you go and, because you have impeccable taste in dress, you will always be lucky in love; even though, as I said, you may choose not to marry young.

Once you choose a family life, you will be extremely protective, perhaps even territorial. You must not let yourself become possessive, however, as this will cause problems in your marital life. When you do find the right person you will be determined and proud of your commitment. Because of this, I can say with confidence that the love life for Leo is generally fulfilling and spiritually enlightening as well.

Health, wellbeing and diet

Few signs have the stamina and the energy that you do, Leo, but this also means that you are likely to push a lot harder, work longer hours and to place a greater strain on your body than others. I suggest therefore that you protect your most valuable assets—your vitality and health—so you can continue to be successful and happy in life.

Because you love sport and outdoor activities, this could be a great asset to maintaining your health, but it can create the exact opposite if you overdo it. Try to be moderate in everything you do and this will augment your health and wellbeing.

Because Leo rules the spine, the back and the heart, these are the areas that may be prone to injury and later in life some type of weakness. Furthermore, pay attention to your posture so that such things as backache and spinal curvature don't become problems as you grow older. Cardiovascular health is also important, so maintain a good diet.

Because Leo is a hot, dry sign of the zodiac, spicy dishes and food that sizzles the palate could be your favourites. You have a quick metabolism, which burns up most of what you eat, and therefore more Leos enjoy eating meat and other heavy foods. This makes sense because the lion is of course a lover of red meat—particularly cooked rare.

You need to eat more wholegrain foods and fresh vegetables to counteract this aspect of your taste. Also, try to avoid processed and alkaline foods, which will neutralise any excess acidity in your body.

Some additional herbs and foods that can be of use to improve your health are lime juice, camomile and fenugreek. These will help you detoxify your body and give you more mental clarity. Papaya, mango, banana and other yellow or gold-coloured fruits are great for Leo, too, because these colours are ruled by the Sun and also contain valuable vitamins and minerals that are in keeping with your personality.

Orange vegetables such as pumpkin are first-rate for your health, and wholegrain rice and other steamed foods will increase your vitality as well.

Work

Your attitude to work is so closely attuned to your self-esteem that it's hard to separate the two. You measure your self-worth by what you achieve in the world and this will make you somewhat of a perfectionist in some areas, yet strangely a little sloppy in others.

You have an incredible capacity to achieve your goals and you are always on the go. You never stop and need to associate yourself with others who are on the same energetic level. You work equally well alone, in a team, or as an employee, when you will be indispensable and highly valued by your employers.

You expect to be paid well for what you do, and it doesn't matter what line of work you choose, for you will be successful. Because of your need for recognition you will enjoy your work, but you must not let your ego dictate some of the decisions you need to make, particularly if you run your own business.

You are not discouraged easily and your determination is such that even an adverse circumstance can be turned into a positive one for you.

You're passionate, extravagant and creative, but you are also able to curb this when you feel the necessity.

You certainly need to be the boss in your line of work and can make an excellent executive, teacher or, with your dramatic flair, someone who can work with great satisfaction in the world of theatre, film or on the stage.

Outdoor activities and sports are a wonderful line of activity for you and so working with the environment, plants and animals is also a good bet as a career.

Your lucky days

Your luckiest days are Mondays, Tuesdays, Thursdays and Sundays.

Your lucky numbers

Remember that the forecasts given later in the book will help you optimise your chances of winning. Your lucky numbers are:

1, 10, 19, 28, 37, 46, 55

3, 12, 21, 30, 39, 48, 57

9, 18, 27, 36, 45, 54, 63

Your destiny years

Your most important years are 1, 10, 19, 28, 37, 46, 55, 64, 73 and 82.

Star Sign Compatibility

If you would create something, you must be something.

—Johann Wolfgang von Goethe

Romantic compatibility

How compatible are you with your current partner, lover or friend? Did you know that astrology can reveal a whole new level of understanding between people simply by looking at their star sign and that of their partner? In this chapter I'd like to share some special insights that will help you better appreciate your strengths and challenges using Sun sign compatibility.

The Sun reflects your drive, willpower and personality. The essential qualities of two star signs blend like two pure colours producing an entirely new colour. Relationships, similarly, produce their own emotional colours when two people interact. The following is a general guide to your romantic prospects with others and how, by knowing the astrological 'colour' of each other, the art of love can help you create a masterpiece.

When reading the following I ask you to remember that no two star signs are ever *totally* incompatible. With effort and compromise, even the most 'difficult' astrological matches can work. Don't close your mind to the full range of life's possibilities! Learning about each other and ourselves is the most important facet of astrology.

Each star sign combination is followed by the elements of those star signs and the result of their combining. For instance, Aries is a fire sign and Aquarius is an air sign, and this combination produces a lot of 'hot air'. Air feeds fire, and fire warms air. In fact, fire requires air. However, not all air and fire combinations work. I have included information about the different birth periods within each star sign and this will throw even more light on your prospects for a fulfilling love life with any star sign you choose.

Good luck in your search for love, and may the stars shine upon you in 2009!

Compatibility quick reference guide

Each of the twelve star signs has a greater or lesser affinity with one another. The quick reference guide on page 30 will show you who's hot and who's not so hot as far as your relationships are concerned.

LEO + ARIES
Fire + Fire = Explosion

I describe the partnership between Leo and Aries as 'a bomb waiting to go off'! A 'love bomb', that is. You see, when two fire signs unite, the result is one of great dynamism, passion and energy and that magnetic attraction is obvious right from the word 'go'.

Fire signs are very driven and ambitious characters, therefore you and your Aries partner will resonate on the same wavelength, supporting each other, sharing many of the same aspirations in life, making a great team.

You are a calm sort of person, Leo, and also project a commanding type of energy around you. Aries has a similar approach to life so they must be prepared to make allowances for the fact that you are very alike in nature. You just have to take turns at being 'the boss'.

There is another possible scenario here with such a fiery and competitive combination: your high level of energy could create a lifestyle that burns out both of you. You might need to be a little more playful with Aries because you will notice much of what you do seems to trigger a response of competitiveness if not sometimes open aggressiveness from your Arian partner.

On a sexual note, the creative expression of your fiery element is a very positive aspect and reflects your compatibility

Quick reference guide: Horoscope compatibility between signs (percentage)

	Aries	Taurus	Gemini	Cancer	Leo	Virgo	Libra	Scorpio	Sagittarius	Capricorn	Aquarius	Pisces
Pisces	65	85	50	90	75	70	50	95	75	85	55	80
Aquarius	55	80	90	70	70	50	95	60	60	70	80	55
Capricorn	50	95	50	45	45	95	85	65	55	85	70	85
Sagittarius	90	50	75	55	95	70	80	80	85	55	60	75
Scorpio	80	85	60	95	75	85	85	90	85	65	60	95
Libra	70	75	90	60	65	80	80	85	80	85	95	50
Virgo	45	90	75	75	75	70	80	85	70	95	50	70
Leo	90	70	80	70	85	75	65	75	95	45	70	75
Cancer	65	80	60	75	70	75	60	95	55	45	70	90
Gemini	65	70	75	60	80	75	90	60	75	50	90	50
Taurus	65	70	70	80	70	90	75	85	50	95	80	85
Aries	60	70	70	65	90	45	70	80	90	50	55	65

in the bedroom on a physical level. You both feel comfortable and demonstrative in your affections. The fire signs need to feel appreciated in these matters and so you both get the thumbs up between the sheets. The nice thing about the Aries–Leo combination is that the spark will continue in your relationship, keeping your love fresh and sparkling.

You are both overindulgent people, so this is one area that you may need to talk about and curb, especially with respect to your finances. You need to make some provisions for a rainy day.

You will be very attracted to Aries born between 21 and 30 March. Being doubly ruled by Mars indicates that your karmic paths are destined to cross. Travelling and study seem to be an important focus of this relationship and I see it as being one full of joy.

Although most Aries will be compatible with you, by far the best are those born between 31 March and 10 April. These Aries individuals have a strong Leo focus and this means you will be instantly drawn to each other because of the very similar personality traits in you. There is an intuitive connection between Leos and this group of Aries and again I can say that this will be an excellent match.

Aries born between 11 and 20 April have a touch of Sagittarius in their makeup as well as that of Aries. This can be a very fulfilling relationship and one that is full of excitement. I see plenty of sexual connectedness for the two of you.

LEO + TAURUS
Fire + Earth = Lava

The rulers of Leo and Taurus are the Sun and Venus, respectively. Astrology usually describes this combination as extremely charming and attractive, offering a healthy dose of sociability for those in whose chart these two planets combine.

Eastern astrologers are not so generous in their interpretation and suggest that these two planets can be at odds with each other.

There is no doubt you will be attracted to Taurus and vice versa; however, once the relationship settles into a groove it will be obvious your personalities are considerably different.

Both of you are what are known as 'thick' signs, which means being rather set in your ways if not stubborn on certain viewpoints. You will find yourselves clashing because of this and you will both need to learn to be more flexible.

You are a protective sort of person and, because Taurus is very much concerned by issues of security, they will be drawn to you for this reason. You offer them confidence and this could be the one saving grace in your relationship. You are also able to bring out the romantic and sexual side of Taurus and it could be said that physically this is quite a good combination.

Socially you are both quite active and as a couple you will make a strong impression and attract many friends. As well as a mutual group of friends, you also choose to maintain your own individual peer group. You must allow each other some independence in this respect.

The relationship may not necessarily be a long-term one, but you can rest assured that it will be sizzling hot. Fire plus earth equals lava!

You must learn to move slowly with Taurus and introduce them to your way of doing things one step at a time. You have very open and dramatic gestures and, if you would learn to temper your behaviour a little so that the patient and plodding Taurus isn't too overwhelmed, you could turn this relationship into something more permanent.

If your Taurus friend is born between 21 and 29 April, they are a seductive character and you will find it hard to resist wanting to know more about them. They are slow-moving and quite opinionated. They have a fixed way of doing things, which could frustrate you. They will not usually change their ways to fit in with who you are.

One of your better partners would be a Taurus born between 30 April and 10 May. They will take interest in your social life and also help in your professional or business life. Mercury, one of the rulers, is strongly linked to your finances and so you can have the best of both worlds—romantically and financially.

There are opportunities for a fulfilling relationship arising with those Taureans born between 11 and 21 May. You both have a common interest in family life and will work hard to satisfy each other's domestic needs. Once that commitment is made it could be the exception to the rule and is a long-term connection.

LEO + GEMINI
Fire + Air = Hot air

You're intrigued by the quirky and mentally stimulating air sign of Gemini. Your fiery energy warms their intellectual element, creating a bubbly, interactive type of relationship. Generally, according to astrologers, this is a wonderful combination that has a great chance of going the distance.

Your social and communicative association will be a special one and you both feed off each other in this respect because of being emotionally in tune with each other.

Because Gemini is one of the flightiest signs of the zodiac, they'll feel drawn to your stability and innate strength. They sense that you're loyal and supportive and this then helps to steady their changeable nature. They feel comfortable talking to you about their problems and often you will be able to show them a different angle, a deeper view of their lives and how they can be a little more practical in solving these issues.

Being the king of the jungle, your leonine nature likes to dominate the surroundings and be centre stage. You are at times a little too strong and inflexible for Gemini, who is scattered yet at the same time flexible in adjusting to your fixity.

You are a creative individual and this also works well with Gemini's versatile mind. Your skills can complement each other and I see much mutual appreciation and admiration for each other.

Gemini has an amazing ability with facts and figures and can impress you with the speed and agility of their mind. You will need to help them focus their attention and, if you can do so, it may work well for you in terms of your own lifelong fulfilment. They can be great supporters of any cause that you aspire to.

Gemini's born between 22 May and 1 June should be regarded as an asset to your business. Apart from being friends, you can draw upon their immense insight and creative, intellectual ideas. Making money together will come naturally to both of you.

A Gemini born between 2 and 12 June will magnetically draw you to them and will fit in well with your social circle. They live and play hard so fortunately the Leo stamina is able to keep up with them. You are both workaholics and because of this you might find it hard to fit into each other's schedules. If you are serious about a relationship with them make sure your actions speak as loudly as your words.

Geminis born between 13 and 21 June are potential marriage partners. This is due to the fact that they are co-ruled by Aquarius, which just so happens to rule your marital sector. You will be attracted to each other and could meet suddenly or in unusual circumstances.

LEO + CANCER

Fire + Water = Steam

It's never a good idea to enter into any relationship with high expectations of somehow pigeonholing the person into a pre-conceived idea of how you want them to be. This line of thinking is particularly damaging if you have to foster a relationship with Cancer.

Cancer is a sensitive sign and, although the Moon, its ruler, is friendly to the Sun, the Moon does tend to get rather weak when in its proximity. This is because the powerful, magnetic vibrations that are reflected in your personality are a little too much for Cancer to take in all at once.

Try not to be too dominating with Cancer, who will respond better to a softer approach if you are trying to make your point.

The alternative explanation of the compatibility between Leo and Cancer is that the Moon represents the feminine principle of nurturing and motherly love, whereas the Sun depicts masculine principles of fiery and aggressive energy. Male–female. You and Cancer seem to perfectly reflect these two essential forces in nature.

Given this is a sensual relationship, on the most fundamental energy level you will be attracted to each other, but by the same token you will need to direct your energies carefully so that the inherent potential of your relationship can develop and flourish.

Cancer is the twelfth sign to Leo in the circle of the zodiac and this indicates a tendency for expenditure in material resources and emotions. Leo is the second sign to Cancer, which augments these areas. Cancer's emotional sensitivity will certainly tire you; yet on the other hand, you will be able to inspire them and uplift their spirits. You might find it hard in dealing with their very changeable and moody nature, which is also another aspect of their being ruled by the Moon.

Try not to dominate them as they need time to settle emotionally before making any decisions. Give them room to breathe and mull over their decisions. Try to get more in tune with the psychic and spiritual energies of Cancer because then you won't feel as though your energy is so diminished.

You have reasonably good romantic opportunities with Cancerians born between 15 and 23 July. They are particularly generous, in keeping with your own magnanimous nature. They are selfless in their emotional demonstrativeness, and you will be drawn to this.

If they are born between 4 and 14 of July, these Cancerians are really stubborn and possibly too emotionally demanding for you. Nevertheless you will still feel some sort of attraction to them and you will enjoy their strong will and purposeful nature, even though they are a little inflexible. You will respect this.

You might find it difficult entering into a relationship with Cancerians born between 22 June and 3 July because you might think their heads are in the clouds. They are probably not as physically motivated as you either and this is something you feel is essential if the relationship is going to be successful.

LEO + LEO
Fire + Fire = Explosion

There is an innate understanding between couples when their elements are the same. This is even more so when the star sign is also the same, as in the case of a relationship between Leo and Leo.

Leo represents willpower, charisma and the ego. These issues will be very much a part of your life lessons if you choose to enter a relationship with another Leo.

No doubt you will be instantaneously attracted to each other; but, once the admiration, praise and initial passion start to settle down, you will soon realise that you each possess very powerful wills and could in fact begin to clash on many different fronts.

You both demand recognition and are comfortable being at the centre of attention. You make no apologies for this but you are dealing with another Leo here so this is an aspect of the relationship that will require very delicate handling.

Notwithstanding this power conflict, you are both bright, even dazzling stars, whose coming together will attract ample opportunities and respect from the world around you. You love to be in the company of others individually and as a unit.

The element of fire, when teaming with another fire sign, can be quite explosive. A moment of tension must not be allowed to get out of hand for this could ruin many good aspects of your relationship. You must both find suitable outlets for showing how you feel, especially if you are angry, so that emotions don't become confused.

As fire signs you are so inherently spiritual. You will be interested in your own personal emotional and intellectual growth and this is where you could be a formidable support for each other.

Both of you have karmic lessons to learn that centre on humility. One of the key phrases that should be considered is 'Let he who has served, command'. This could bring an opportunity for you both to experience love at the deepest level.

You must not let the superficial aspect of how you look and how you are seen by the public to overtake the spiritual, sensible elements of this relationship. It is easy for Leo to get caught up in the whirlwind of social glamour, which would be a shame for a relationship that has so much going for it.

Leos born between 24 July and 4 August are extremely obstinate and possibly a bit hard for the majority of Leos to deal with. It's an inflexible combination, so learning to adjust to each other's needs will be one of the challenges of the relationship.

Leos born between 5 and 14 August are a less dominant type and they have a very honest and open path. Both friendship and humour are parts of their nature. You will enjoy that.

For those Leos wanting a relationship with others born between 15 and 23 August, you can expect some pretty intense clashes of will. This is the most complex group but will probably attract other Leos. There is a somewhat unstable and unpredictable outcome for a relationship with them.

LEO + VIRGO
Fire + Earth = Lava

There are two ways this relationship can go, and hopefully when I speak of the importance of communication, it would be the path of open, honest and clear and decisive discussion. The other, God forbid, is a cloudy mess of confusing ideas, which trip up both of you.

In this partnership it is important for you, Leo, to understand that Virgo is shy and sometimes unassuming; but don't mistake this for character weakness. You must give Virgo a chance to shine their intellectual light, which is equal to, and maybe even better than, your own.

Virgo is precise in its analysis of life and in particular in its relationships with others, so you should be prepared to find yourself often under their scrutinising microscope. This will unnerve you as the penetrating insights of Virgo will start to reveal some of your own flaws. But this is not a bad thing, is it?

Aren't relationships supposed to be about self-improvement, lifting yourself to a standard that represents the best you can be?

Virgo is concerned with details, whereas you are what we might refer to as a 'big picture' person. Here again are some differences in your style, in your approach to life generally.

You want to be the centre of attention, whereas Virgo is quite content to be in the background. Now, this aspect of the relationship will suit you down to the ground and is probably one of the great strengths of the Leo–Virgo combination.

Virgo is also a little cool in the bedroom (to start with, that is). Once you work your way into their hearts, they will love your passionate, warm and endearing leonine temperament. You will soon realise that Virgo is not as virginal as everyone might expect and can surprise you with just how much they are capable of giving.

If you find yourself attracted to a Virgo born between 23 August and 2 September, you will be pleased to note that they are not quite as nervy as your typical Virgo. They will defend you quickly and you can share some really great times with them. They will open up to your Leo personality and this relationship could be quite special.

Virgos born between 3 and 12 September are fairly straight down the line and this is to do with the influence of Saturn on them. You will need to work hard to bring them out of their shell and they are not typically as spontaneous as you would like your partners to be.

You will be very attracted to Virgos born between 13 and 23 September. In getting to know them you will find that their dominating personalities do tend to clash with yours. You will have to curtail some of your domineering ways if you want this relationship to be a success.

LEO + LIBRA

Fire + Air = Hot air

The key component of your relationship with Libra would be to inspire and motivate each other to achieve as much as possible.

Libra is an air sign ruled by Venus, which makes them particularly charming, sociable and clever. Unlike you, they may not need to always take centre stage to prove their worth. The air element is also a little hard to catch hold of and in the proximity of a warm fire can move even more quickly.

You can share large doses of happiness, adventure and optimism in your relationship. Looking and feeling great is a common interest and you will be a handsome couple, impeccable in terms of colour, harmony and general etiquette.

Librans are very diplomatic characters and, when you look at their totem, their scales of justice, you quickly realise that this perfectly represents their personality. They avoid arguments and dislike any sort of disruption or crass behaviour. Their natural philosophy in life is one of peace and harmony. You must never take advantage of this and disregard their need for balance as they won't stand for it.

As long as you are respectful and, if possible, calm and collected in your differences of opinion, they will be happy to accept you graciously. If on the other hand you make a show of your strength and try to crush them, it will definitely backfire.

Librans will appreciate your direct brand of honesty and openness. This is akin to their ideas of justice and fair play. Libra's mind will astound you because their gems of intellectual brilliance are like a multi-faceted diamond. You can learn much about peace and harmony in your relationship with them.

A powerful attraction is likely between you and Libra, though, because both of you have ample charisma, which seems to connect together easily. It is a lucky combination as well and, if you choose to work hard as a partnership, you will acquire both material and spiritual blessings.

You have common interests in such things as parties, dinners and other functions, but the hub of your life will certainly be your domestic arena, which will be the focal point for much fun and social activities. You both take pride in having friends and like to make them part of your lives.

There is a strong karmic relationship with Librans born between 4 and 13 October. They are slightly crazy in their attitude, but you will be attracted to them and love their spontaneity and independence.

Librans born between 24 September and 3 October are also well suited to you. They are always on the go and if you are happy to be persistently in motion with them, you will enjoy hanging out with them.

Generally Librans born between 14 and 23 October are only moderately compatible with you. Mercury, a changeable planet, co-rules them and their shifting moods may not be to your liking.

LEO + SCORPIO
Fire + Water = Steam

You can't handle anyone who is insipid, weak or wishy-washy and so your meeting with Scorpio will naturally bring a smile to your face. You'll feel an immediate respect for the strong-willed Scorpio, which I might add is one of a few star signs that can match your own with willpower and self-confidence.

With a matching of your powers, you will find Scorpio determined, purposeful and persistent. You will test each other's will and neither of you is a pushover, as you will soon learn.

The fire and water combination of your star signs could result in a pressure-cooker environment over time, especially in matters of sexual gratification. There is an intensely emotional vibe to the Scorpio personality and only the most evolved Leo can deal with it. If you are able to pat yourself on the back and say 'Yes, I fit the bill', then you may have just found yourself a mate for life in Scorpio.

Bill Clinton and Hillary are the perfect example of the Leo–Scorpio couple, who were able to surmount their turbulent relationship difficulties against all odds. Yes, when Bill was in power Hillary was his rock, through thick and thin. While Hillary was aiming for the top job, the roles were reversed and he has supported her as much as she did him. This is an example of the incredibly strong bond that the Leo and Scorpio couple can develop.

Scorpio is philosophical, psychological and seeks knowledge, which is deep and complex. Don't even bother if this sort of stuff is too scary for you. In any case, Scorpio will soon understand whether or not your mind is capable of joining with theirs to develop this relationship in ways that are extraordinary.

Scorpios born between 3 and 12 November are very well suited to your temperament. If you are born between 4 and 15 August, this compatibility is even greater. For other Leo-born individuals, this might not be such a great match, so I don't recommend long-term or committed relationships with them.

Most Scorpios are not necessarily open about their taste for control and power but that is part and parcel of their character, have no doubt about that. You also like to assert your will but that would be the wrong move, especially with Scorpios born between 13 and 22 November. This group of Scorpios isn't quite as difficult and complex as the typical Scorpio. You must learn to accommodate their sensitive and spiritual temperament if you are to foster this relationship.

Any Scorpios born between 24 October and 2 November are particularly magnetic and intense. Their sexual appetites are very strong and so you will be more than happy to be seduced by them. I see this as a very good combination, indeed.

LEO + SAGITTARIUS
Fire + Fire = Explosion

As far as relationships are concerned I have to say that this is a pretty hard combination to beat. Each of you radiates warmth, power and mutual love, which are what your element of fire is all about.

Sagittarius is almost like yourself and sometimes blunt in their manner, but that's okay by you; you are thick-skinned enough to handle this direct type of attitude.

There is a karmic connection between you and Sagittarius and, from the moment you begin speaking with them for the first time, it will be as if you are connecting with a long-lost friend. You tend to reflect each other's enthusiasm for life and enjoy this immensely. You are both very straightforward and also passionate in your feelings for each other.

Because Sagittarius relates to travel and the excitement of discovery, they stimulate you to do the same. If you are a Leo that has been stuck in some sort of rut, developing a relationship with Sagittarius will put an end to it. You better have your bags packed ready for the numerous adventures that are likely to happen if you team up with your Sagittarian counterpart! This will keep your relationship alive and the omens are great for a long-term partnership.

Sagittarius is often free and easy in its approach to life, and you may demand a little more in the way of commitment from them than they initially lead you to believe they are capable of. Bide your time, however, as they need the stability of Leo's influence to make them feel complete.

Both of you are energetic and enthusiastic about life. Even though Sagittarius is somewhat easygoing, there is an unspoken understanding between you and you generally adapt quite easily to each other's day-to-day routines and lifestyles.

Because the fire signs are so creative, you will spark and bounce off each other's ideas, injecting life and inspiration into each other. You can extend this to your sexual lives as well, and this should be no less invigorating and spontaneous. You are both interested in keeping your relationship fresh and alive. This is certainly one of the best sexual combinations in the zodiac.

Sagittarians born between 12 and 22 December have a deep emotional connection with you because they too are partly ruled by the Sun and Leo. You can truly be yourself with them and in fact will find them drawing out of you the best part of your personality and character.

I can safely predict a very exciting love affair with a Sagittarian born between 23 November and 1 December. Their passion is extremely strong and their personalities intense. This is a perfect match for your fiery and ardent love. Your physical relationship will be the highlight of this particular combination.

Your relationship with any Sagittarian born between 2 and 11 December is strongly rooted in your karmic memories. The spiritual association will help you get through some of this life's lessons together. They could be instrumental in radically transforming your life in some way.

LEO + CAPRICORN
Fire + Earth = Lava

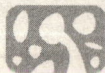

If you are a Leo that likes a long-shot and are game enough to take a gamble in relationships, then you might want to try your hand with Capricorn.

The two of you are essentially very different people: you being ruled by the bright, warm solar disc called the Sun and Capricorn by the cool and sober Saturn. You really are quite at odds with each other when we look at your personalities.

You have a keen desire to radiate, communicate and interact with as many people as you can. Capricorn for the most part finds this a little difficult; at least initially, until the trust factor is overcome. They are more introverted and solitary and prefer to do things in a low-key manner. You actively seek recognition and as much attention as possible in what you do.

I am sure you can see that both of you are poles apart in your character, and making a relationship work would indeed be a long-shot, as I have warned. Your contrasting energies can work together, but the compromises would be extremely large— possibly too large for the average Leo and Capricorn to make.

One area you may find considerably difficult is in matters of intimacy and sex. You both approach this private aspect of your lives as differently as your personalities are. Capricorn is conservative and seeks considerable security as an end result, whereas you're happier to enjoy the moment and creatively, spontaneously push the relationship to the limits in the now.

Capricorns born between 2 and 10 January will possibly offer you a little more than the typical Capricorn we have been talking about, particularly in their affectionate responses to you. As I said, many Capricorns tend to be conservative, especially sexually. But once you get to know this group you will uncover a whole spectrum of character traits that you might not have anticipated. It is well worth persisting with these Capricorns and, who knows, some magic might just happen.

With Capricorns born between 23 December and 1 January, the differences could be way too stark for you to handle. These Capricorns are quite aloof and certainly too cool for your taste. They are very cautious, security conscious and definitely not as spontaneous as you. They may also find it difficult opening up and sharing their feelings with you. You have a long, hard climb trying to win them over because of these marked differences.

There is a great intellectual rapport between you and Capricorns born between 11 and 20 January. You could be good friends and, as well, may be able to put your heads together and come up with unusual professional and financial solutions, especially if you both have an interest in business. This group too may be an exception to the Leo–Capricorn rule.

LEO + AQUARIUS
Fire + Air = Hot air

It is not always correct to say that 'opposites attract' and, in astrology when two star signs happen to be opposite each other, as in this case, there are some exceptions to that rule. There are two extreme possibilities here; that is, it can either work well or be a disastrous waste of time.

This will all depend on how developed you both are and how receptive to each other's needs you happen to be. That Aquarius is an air sign and you a fire sign is not necessarily that bad, elementally. Aquarius has a quiet and intellectual curiosity that could balance your larger-than-life attitude. You are spontaneous and sometimes outspoken and this bubbly aspect of your nature might in time warm the cockles of the Aquarian heart.

You must understand that, although Aquarius does tend to seem somewhat detached at times, they are in fact quite revolutionary in their attitudes and will surprise you once they feel comfortable enough to reveal some of their own shock tactics.

The two of you do have some common similarities in that you are both strong-willed and a little self-absorbed as well. Aquarius will have opinions that are just as strong and inflexible as your own. This could become a battleground, especially if you both take interest in social, religious or political subjects. I can see many confrontational episodes unless you are prepared to respect each other's differences.

There are some Leos that are conservative and, with Aquarius being as aggressive as they are, they may not respect the conventional approach that you prefer.

If you are thinking of bedding down for the long-haul with an Aquarian, you need to be adventurous, high-spirited and, of course, flexible enough to trust that where they want to take the relationship may be a completely different direction to what you had at first envisioned.

If you are looking for a marital partner or at least a long-term relationship, Aquarians born between 21 and 30 January will probably stimulate you enough to keep your interest. Even though you may have some basic differences, this is something that can be smoothed over with trial and error.

Aquarians born between 31 January and 8 February are friendly characters and have a need to share their inner thoughts and experiences. As long as you are a good listener and are prepared to offer them centre stage from time to time, I see you both being well suited romantically.

By far your best match with an Aquarian would have to be with those born between 9 and 19 February. They are staunchly loyal supporters of whatever it is you want to achieve and won't necessarily compete with you. There is a good synergy between you and Aquarians born during this period.

LEO + PISCES
Fire + Water = Steam

You have to guide your Piscean friend slowly into the world of commerce and the rat-race in general. You will have a way of inspiring Pisces on a practical level, while in turn, spiritually they can do the same for you. Let me explain.

Pisces is the final sign of the twelve zodiac signs and is considered by many to be the most evolved and spiritual astrologically. The Sun, your ruler, is also essentially spiritual in nature but has yet to absorb some of the more refined influences of Pisces. If you are open enough to this, this could be an exceptional foundation for a long-term relationship. If, however, this is not the case, I see some struggles between you and the super-sensitive Pisces.

Pisces is concerned with selflessness whereas Leo is concerned with self. While you are busy trying to inflate your ego and to develop your strength of mind and purpose in life, Pisces in its own way will be slowly negating all of this, similar to one step forward and two steps backward. It is simply a difference of perspective.

Tolerance and patience are the best key words to suggest in your relationship with Pisces. Your patience will pay off when you realise that there is so much that can be shared between you and you can have a wonderful love life together.

Pisces needs your leadership and direction and will soon get the hang of what it is like to achieve things in the world. Their self-esteem will grow considerably through a relationship with you and, especially if the Pisces we are talking about is the shy and nervy type, you will see some dramatic changes in their personality through their association with you.

They will be able to act as a sort of spiritual counsellor for you. They will help you get in touch with the deeper emotional aspects of your being and, if you happen to be a little sceptical about psychic topics, you might be surprised to find that your intuition will start to develop under their mateship.

One of my favourite sayings is that 'If you're too busy looking at the log of wood in the other man's eye, you will miss the splinter of glass in your own'. This is an old Mediterranean saying, which warns you against too much fault-finding with Pisces. They are sensitive individuals who need encouragement and support from a strong-willed Leo, remember that.

Your emotional and sexual energies are quite out of the ordinary and may not initially gel. Where there is a will there is a way, and you certainly have enough willpower—that I don't doubt. Pisces is the eighth zone to Leo, which is the region of sexuality. Strangely, you may have some exciting sexual interaction with Pisces, believe it not.

Pisces born between 20 and 28 or 29 February are a difficult match for Leos and, even though there is a strong sexual connection for you, your practical life just won't be that compatible.

Pisces born between 1 and 10 March are sensitive and responsive individuals and these are aspects of them to which you will be drawn. They are particularly spiritual and imaginatively motivated and can't necessarily express what they feel. This is where your patience will be absolutely necessary.

Any Piscean individual born between 11 and 20 March might turn out to be a good match for you. They are fierier than their other Pisces brothers and sisters. These Pisces have a Scorpio element to their nature and this makes them extremely passionate and demonstrative, which is something you will enjoy immensely.

2009:
The Year Ahead

Happy are those who dream dreams and are ready to pay the price to make them come true.

—Leon J. Suenes

Romance and friendship

A rare phenomenon occurs for Leo in 2009. Jupiter passing through your zone of love and marriage occurs early in January and represents a rare opportunity for you to find new meaning in your relationships. This influence occurs only once in twelve years, so make the most of it.

This is certainly an exciting time for you, a year where you can feel genuinely optimistic about your current friendships, love affairs or marriage. If you do not yet have a partner, you can feel quietly confident that it's only a matter of time before Mr or Mrs Right comes along.

Let me assure you, with Mercury and Jupiter combining their lucky energies in this department of your life, your communication and your ability to impress others by your mere presence, will not be without positive and very fulfilling results.

You seem to have your finger on the pulse this year and you won't have to go too far away to find love. You are very much like a magnet, drawing people to you, even in the usual day-to-day places you might otherwise not expect to find anything special happening. That is not to say that you won't be lured into some adventurous forays interstate or even overseas, which is very likely for the purpose of fulfilling your emotional desires throughout late February early March where Venus enters your zone of long-distance journeys.

During February, your sharp tongue may get you into hot water, though, as Mercury and Mars stir up dissatisfaction in the area of long-term relationships. You might find yourself travelling without your partner if you don't control your energies.

You make your power felt, but you kind of stomp on the ones you love. This is not the way to direct these forceful energies.

You will be feeling far more independent and self-reliant and will need to be assured that your position in love is at least that of an equal if not superior.

If you are a Leo who happens to be in a possessive relationship, this may also bring you into conflict with your spouse or partner. Your need will be to expand your circle of friends and to develop associations with others who will help you grow emotionally, mentally and spiritually. Nothing will stop you from getting out and connecting with many interesting people.

Up to the 12th of March, your life will be hectic and almost seem like things are moving fast forward, with Uranus and the Sun accelerating your lifestyle. Suppression of any sort will be unwise, but by the same token you must curb your tendency towards restlessness and instability.

If you are looking for friendship or a more stable relationship, this may not be the best time for you to make commitments, as your freedom and independence will be a priority.

Contacts with strangers or unusual people in April are profitable. It's always easy to imagine that someone you don't know has all the answers and is your ticket to a better lifestyle, or a more fulfilling relationship, but you know that's not exactly reality. Keep your expectations real this year, because all that glitters is not gold. Throughout April you may want to treat yourself lavishly to many social engagements, festivities and parties. If you plan to live for the moment, that's okay, as long as you keep in mind the consequences of your actions.

Neptune will create some doubts for you throughout the period of May to August, so you must make sure that your thinking is systematic and your judgement of others practical. This is the time when you need to be perfectly honest with yourself and talk about how you feel. There is no use living a dream in your mind if the life situation you are in is anything but fulfilling.

Jupiter and Neptune combined with the hard aspect of Mercury cause your communications to be caught up in gridlock—differences of opinion, incompatible philosophies and generally a problem in meeting friends and lovers halfway.

If you are dissatisfied with your life, try talking about this to someone who has a sympathetic ear and if necessary lay low for a while and don't superimpose these dissatisfactions on the ones you love. It is easy to project our fears and apprehensions on others while in fact the problems stem from deep within us.

In the last few days of May your energy will be recovered and you will feel much more settled in yourself, especially if you choose to find an outlet for your raw energy through vigorous sports and other outdoor activities. You will also find more meaning in your work that will take pressure off your personal relationships.

You will begin to feel irritable in June when Mars challenges your Sun sign. If you have been fortunate enough to develop a lifestyle in which sport, good diet and friendly, open competition is part of the mix, this will not present any problems and will in fact be a fun time. Picnics, barbeques, beach days and trips to the country are ideal ways to let off steam and build closer emotional bonds with friends.

When the Sun returns to its birth position, you will feel a lift in your self-esteem and your ability to attract the right sort of people into your life. This happens in August and continues somewhat into September with the presence of lucky and seductive Venus in your Sun sign as well. These two months will be thoroughly enjoyable, bringing you instant recognition wherever you go and the likelihood of many new friends, too.

Be careful of your communications throughout September, however, because Mercury in its retrogressed movement may create difficulties and misunderstandings in discussions. Clarify what is said so that you don't end up dealing with others in a blame game. By October many of these issues will be cleared up.

Excellent planetary aspects occur in October and present you with opportunities to creatively achieve the things you would like in your love life. The Moon and Neptune with Jupiter are very auspicious and this is the time where you will meet the love of your life if you are as yet unattached. Venus and Mercury also offer you strong support and your communication will be matched by someone special who takes interest in your mental as well as physical qualities. That's rare these days, but such is the luck of Leo in 2009.

Jupiter, which has reference to your love affairs, makes an important impact upon you around the middle of October and many of your misconceptions or misunderstandings with a loved one will mysteriously evaporate.

The movement of Mercury to your zone of family and domestic happiness in the last couple of days of the month is also auspicious in reconciling with relatives, particularly your mother, if you are bothered by any long-standing issues.

I see big hopes, big dreams arising before you in November and, depending on your faith in yourself, these can and will be implemented as well. If you are overenthusiastic or exceedingly ambitious in your expectation you may find yourself having to coax someone to think as loudly and big as you do. Remember, not everyone has the same level of confidence or sees the horizon as clearly as you can.

Children may be an issue for you in the last part of the year so you will need to handle them with skill and love. Under no circumstances entertain the notion that arguing with youngsters is going to produce a solution. If your children are still in your care, sidestep these head-on confrontations and stand firm as the parent and the boss of the house. This will work wonders and create instant domestic peace for you.

You may be feeling a little cool in your emotions throughout October and November, but this is all part of the process of developing your insight and shedding your past conceptions about 'how a relationship should be'. I see you learning many new things and growing as a result.

Jupiter remains in your marriage zone throughout the whole of 2009 and has protective influences on all of your personal relationships; so don't worry if the odd lull in your enthusiasm for romance occurs. These are all excellent testimonies for an extremely successful and happy time for you.

Venus, the Sun and Mercury forecast even greater happiness that you will experience through your romantic associations in 2009. As they pass through your fifth zone of love affairs, I see your creative impulses getting stronger and inspiring you to move forward into 2010 with a sense of awe and anticipation.

The Moon also transcends its best side at the start of December, which indicates your emotions will gain steadiness and practical fulfilment.

In short, I think 2009 is Leo's lucky year for love.

Work and money

Coincidentally, the influence of Mercury and Jupiter on your zone of partnerships favourably influences your professional life and any of those interactions that require you to deal with the public this year. For this reason you can expect better than normal reactions from others in all areas of your work—sales, employment opportunities, and generally workplace relations with your employers and co-workers.

The early part of the year is quite hectic and, if you are the typical Leo who enjoys dealing with others, being busy and generally putting things forward with great gusto, you will enjoy January. If not, and you are somewhat of a unique Leo-born individual, you might be simply overwhelmed by the sheer volume of calls and demands that might be placed upon you. Simply grin and bear it because that won't do you any harm.

In February, when Mars favourably influences your working zone, you will be making extra efforts to cut through your workload. You will have more energy and vitality than you usually do, but must be careful not to burn the candle at both ends. It's likely you will do this and may suffer a crash; health-wise, that is. Maintain high productivity levels but be balanced in your approach to everything you do. Remember the happy medium.

The pace of your life continues and balancing your personal and professional responsibilities could be difficult throughout March. You may be more competitive as well and this could cause some issues for you if your success invites envy from some of your close peers. Try to be humble in your approach as this will minimise damage on the work-front.

Throughout the year Saturn continues to make a strong impression upon you with respect to your finances. This year is a year where you are more frugal and resourceful. Whereas in the past your philosophy was more is better, you will find that this is quite the opposite in 2009. Saving and becoming more aware of the need for future security will prompt you to be less wasteful in all areas of your life. As a result your savings balance will grow.

Your efforts to achieve success will meet less resistance after April when you will be able to achieve a new position through enlisting a friend's support. Whatever projects you are working on are likely to get a green light and your employers will be behind you 100 per cent. Expect some successes, but only if you are prepared to take the odd risk or two.

Between March and August, redefining your career objective will be important. Talking to employment advisers, recruitment officers and maybe even career psychologists wouldn't be a bad idea to help you get a clearer perspective on what sorts of jobs would better suit your personality.

If you feel as if you are in a dead-end role it would be an opportunity that would lead you out of the maze of confusion. Even if you are earning a good salary, you may find that the creative challenge is no longer there and it could be time for you to take a gamble and make that all-important change.

There are sudden career changes around June for some Leos. You'll want something that's progressive and out of the norm. Your mind will be much more original and prepared to take risks. A job change now could offer you something that you have never done before.

Moving into a completely different line of work will be exciting but challenging, but make sure you cross your t's and dot your i's well before jumping ship.

If you desire a leadership position, July could be the time that a promotion is likely. Because of your continued competitive streak, you are likely to win out against your competitors.

You can make excellent progress in September and October and your career objectives will underpin many of your activities. More responsibility will be added to your plate, but I suspect you will be ready for this and even willing to accept more than is offered.

Earlier I said that the challenge may be in leaving the role that some Leos have been working in so far, but now some new skills will be necessary and this will re-invigorate you to proceed with a more cheerful attitude towards your work.

You may find that it's appropriate to lean on a mentor or someone who has trodden your path before. They will be instrumental in helping you further your career ambitions at this time.

In the last few months of the year Venus and Mercury increase your opportunity to earn money. October is one such month in which you may be pleasantly surprised at a pay rise or windfall. Use these new earnings wisely. At this time I also see opportunities to wager a bet and earn extra cash when Venus transits your zone of speculation.

There seems to be a close link between pleasure, gambling and extra income in the closing months of 2009. Enjoy!

Karma, luck and meditation

The fortunate planets for Leo are Jupiter and Mars, and both of these bring ample karmic rewards to you in 2009.

Jupiter in particular indelibly stamps its mark on your emotional and romantic life in the coming twelve months. You may not understand the mechanics of karma, but you will no doubt feel a distinct shift into a better style of relationship and internally a spiritual fulfilment through your marriage or friendships in general. Jupiter has a reputation, especially for Leo, in being a first-rate benefactor.

Mars focuses its auspicious powers upon you in February and March when joining Jupiter in your marriage zone. You may be prone to arguments and confrontation, but generally this is an optimistic and benevolent combination, bringing luck and marriage in some cases.

Expect a good first quarter of 2009, Leo. The Moon and Jupiter bring you further luck in April when they introduce you to friends who wish to help and support you in your future life directions. Someone with a magnanimous spirit, a helper (you may even want to call this person an angel in disguise) will spend much more time with you, helping you clear some of life's obstacles and bring an all-round sense of good luck in your life.

In June and July, Venus in conjunction with Mars promises a lot of passion, possibly through work-related activities. You'll feel happy being yourself and this is one of your greatest strengths in 2009. Others will admire you and be happy to be in your company. It appears that the good deeds of your past are now coming full circle, bringing you only dreamed of results and without much effort on your part, I must say.

Good luck in 2009.

LEO

2009: Month by Month Predictions

Nothing can stop the man with the right mental attitude from achieving his goal; nothing on Earth can help the man with the wrong mental attitude.

—Thomas Jefferson

Highlights of the month

If you are able to understand the deeper significance of astrology and I show you your horoscope for the coming year, you will be astounded at just how fortunate the planets are for you in the coming twelve months. In particular, January is a special time for most Leos due to the important transit of Jupiter into your zone of marriage and intimate personal relationships.

On the 6th, when Jupiter activates this part of your life, you will feel an uplifting in your overall confidence and satisfaction in one-on-one relationships. If you are married, this will be the start of a new cycle where you and your partner can achieve new heights in the relationship.

If you have been working at improving things on the home front, in intimate moments, you will be pleased at just how easily the connection and the communication flow.

Fortunate meetings that seem heaven-sent are likely and, in particular when the Sun moves to the same position as Jupiter after the 20th, this part of your life will be even more accentuated.

Venus and Neptune certainly show just how idealistic you are during this phase and, while you won't be prepared to accept anything less than the highest of standards, try to be a little realistic in your choices. Not everyone aspires to be on the pedestal you may be creating for them and, of course, being human, a few of these people are apt to fall at some time.

Financially, you will continue to be careful about how you spend your money because this first part of the year may indicate a re-appraisal of your financial objectives. This will be particularly so until the middle of the year when you will get a clearer picture of your long-term economic status and security.

Watch your debts in the first couple of weeks, because the Sun and Mars tend to stimulate your appetite for new experiences and wasteful pleasures. You may not necessarily need the things you wish to purchase, so consider second thoughts before madly handing over your credit cards.

Spend some time helping relatives, even though this may be thrust upon you due to the poor health of someone on your mother's side sometime after the 23rd. If you have your schedule in order, you may not be too badly affected by re-adjusting your diary to accommodate a few of the simpler needs.

Try to take more control of your emotions between the 28th and the 30th because you are likely to say or do something that you will regret. You'll want to finish the month on a good note so that you are emotionally disentangled for a good start in February.

Romance and friendship

Don't let pride get in the way of your relationships on the 5th. You probably know someone is thinking of you, so take the first step and take a new friendship to the next level.

On the 7th you're overlooking some of the friends that really care about you and the onus is on you to show how much you value friendships.

You can really enjoy the company of your spouse or partner, particularly after the 11th of the full Moon. It could be during an occasion where their reaction will surprise you but maintaining an optimistic outlook will smooth over any tensions that arise.

On the 15th, attend to that e-mail or letter that you have been postponing writing. If you do have something unpleasant to say there are diplomatic ways in which to sweeten your words so that the outcome is a win–win for all.

On the 18th you may be pointing the finger in the wrong direction, especially if you think you've made an enemy. You're probably your own worst enemy just now and it's not anyone else's fault. Re-examine the intensity of your words and you'll understand what I'm talking about.

If you imagine that you want to be somewhere other than where you are you'll need to back up your vision with some purposeful actions on the 25th and 26th. I'm talking particularly about your residence, your home life and family situation. It's no use daydreaming if you aren't going to make your dreams a reality.

Your personal opinions, particularly regarding your fashion statements, may be of concern to those of your peer group, so dress tastefully on the 30th as this could be the source of a problem. Although your opinions may differ, you still need to respect their viewpoints as well.

Work and money

Your financial concerns are unfounded on the 7th and 8th. The bills you are expecting won't be as bad as you thought; however, don't spend what you don't have.

Your excitement is justified as new opportunities are on the horizon, but don't lose your cool in the process, particularly around the 12th. You might say or do something that is irrational and this will work against your best interests.

Your charitable deeds will not go unnoticed on the 18th, so do your Good Samaritan act quietly and without fanfare. The universe has its own way of thanking you or repaying you for a kind word or deed, but don't necessarily expect this to be in the form of cash.

You could be emotionally strung out on the 23rd due to workplace commitments and things not going quite the way you had planned. Life has its own way of scheduling events and balancing the pros and cons.

You can be imaginative and even playful with your finances after the 28th. This will work better than you expect and may even enhance your business associations as well.

Destiny dates

Positive: 6, 11, 12, 18, 20, 25, 26

Negative: 15, 18, 23, 29, 30

Mixed: 5, 7, 8, 18, 28

Highlights of the month

A lunar eclipse takes place just after the full moon of the 9th and represents a turning point for you in terms of your self-awareness and attitudes to others generally. In fact, on the 10th when the eclipse takes place, you will be struggling with some facet of your personality.

Try to adjust to the way the world sees you as opposed to the way you want to present yourself. If you can spend some time in meaningful analyses of this, you will crack open this nut and find yourself much wiser for it. These insights will help you not just personally, but professionally and spiritually, too.

Some of your wisdom may be gained through the assistance of a mentor, an older and wiser friend who can help you open the doors to this deeper self-awareness. Your thirst for knowledge increases as Venus traverses your zone in the areas of higher knowledge and cultural pursuits.

You will be excited about new information that is coming to light and I dare say you will have ample opportunity to share these gems of wisdom in a social context. It is through this avenue of research and study that new relationships may be fostered in February.

Trust your instincts, follow your dreams and see where it leads you. Particularly from the 12th to the 22nd these activities will be highlighted and you will enjoy many a good conversation with friends and newcomers to your social scene as well. I see several new introductions between the 23rd and the 26th and this will further stimulate your interest in things beyond what you can simply see, hear and touch.

Mercury and Mars bring some nuisance value with their association this month and in your workplace you will have to try especially hard to bite your tongue in response to some of the comments that will be aimed at you.

If you are not able to manage your reactions, you can anticipate more and more head-on confrontations with someone who feels they know better than you. On the 19th and again on the 27th, bite your tongue, take ten deep breaths if necessary, and don't get drawn into any type of open conflicts.

Some new financial opportunities arise after the new Moon of the 26th. If this is not an additional source of income, you can look forward to resolving some differences with your partner if you share the same kitty or have been having issues over who spends what and when.

I detect a little possessiveness associated with your financial interactions this month. Try to see things from the other person's perspective if you can.

Romance and friendship

Some new eye-opening information comes to light on the 2nd. Diplomacy will be necessary, especially with a friend or colleague. Secrecy will be all-important if you are to maintain good relations with your peers. Confidentiality will be your key word throughout the 4th to the 7th.

It's likely you'll be very anxious to try out something new on the 9th but this pathway requires caution, especially if you haven't planned sufficiently. Expect the unexpected.

There's a danger of overestimating the character of someone you meet on the 11th. This could be a younger dark-haired person who crosses your path and may initially seem enthralling, exciting and passionate. I suggest you read between the lines before getting too excited about the situation.

You're fired up and ready for love on the 17th; however, your partner may not be quite as motivated (if you know what I mean). Be careful also not to invite the envy of those around you who aren't feeling quite as attractive or motivated as you. Be careful of run-ins with friends on the 19th and 20th.

A little quiet time will be preferred around the 24th and 25th to re-orientate yourself towards your future emotional goals. You may be tempted to party and socialise around the 26th but your inner self will tell you otherwise.

Take care not to say 'yes' to too many people on the 28th. Set your own agenda and don't let your friends dictate the terms of your schedule because you really do know what is best for you.

On the 29th you have a stronger sense of family and this cycle indicates a serious re-evaluation of your priorities on the domestic front. This will be a time to reignite the bonds of love with your relatives, some of whom you may have ignored for a while.

Work and money

Too much attention may not be all that it is cut out to be around the 2nd. You may regret advertising your services or talents and might feel inundated or smothered by the demands of others. You'll need to escape, especially by the 6th, when you'll preferably want to leave by the back door and give yourself some quality time out.

Don't rush things on the 10th as financial impulses could cause you to stumble, if not fall. Get a better knowledge of the transaction or the business at hand and remember all that glitters is not gold.

Serious concerns on the work front between the 19th and 21st might dampen your otherwise enthusiastic approach and slow your pace. Also, curb your speech as Mercury and Mars could cause you to enter into the odd stoush or two.

You can use a social contact between the 22nd and 24th to extend your commercial influence. There will be several people who can help you achieve your goals quickly but you may have overlooked their willingness to do so.

Enjoyable discussions are likely on the 27th and this could open doors to new business associations.

Destiny dates

Positive: 12, 13, 14, 15, 16, 18, 22, 23, 24, 25, 29

Negative: 11, 28

Mixed: 2, 4, 5, 6, 7, 9, 10, 17, 19, 20, 21, 26, 27

Highlights of the month

Mercury and Mars appear to be transiting through each of your life's departments this month and now they will challenge you in your personal life. Someone who is otherwise cool-headed and rational in their approach will be less than reasonable in their demands. It seems as though you have a continued challenge to manage your feelings and responses.

On the 3rd and 4th, your social appetites are strong, but things can get bogged down when you feel these activities are becoming a little humdrum and superficial. A close friend could make some excessive demands on you but bear in mind you don't always have to give a reason for your choices in life.

From the 7th to the 10th, you have an opportunity to revisit your past or examine that part of your history which is influencing your present circumstances. By understanding your past and the people who coloured your thoughts, opinions and indeed your character, you can gain a tremendous understanding of your present-day relationships.

The full Moon on the 11th and then the new Moon on the 26th spotlight your interests in travel. If you don't actually purchase a ticket to travel, you will be doing an awful lot of daydreaming about faraway places and exotic moments you would like to enjoy.

I always advise that one's life fulfilment comes from the careful blend of creative visualisation, purposeful action and careful planning. Unless you are able to execute these desires, what's the point?

A Herculean effort at adjusting your workload may be necessary after the 18th. You must not avoid the opportunity to put in the extra hours and come up the other end with a big tick next to your name. Your employers will be observing your work skills and commitment to your job at this time. You can and will come out on top.

If you are to have a blow up in your love life, it is likely to occur during the period of the 21st to the 24th. Be increasingly vigilant not to get drawn into backstabbing and of course retrospective blaming. Stick to the point at hand and never attack another personally. These few points will ensure that you come out of this month wiser and emotionally unscathed.

Romance and friendship

Discussions with friends needn't turn into a heated argument on the 3rd and 4th, and these head-on confrontations can be avoided if you take what's being said with a grain of salt. On the 6th don't superimpose your imagination on what you hear.

An appointment or an awaited date that has been rescheduled may have to be changed yet again on the 11th. Welcome the extra time to clear up some other personal matters and catch up on some rest. More often than not the universe plans things perfectly, even if it doesn't seem so at first.

If you're uncomfortable about changes, especially moving house, you may want to reconsider after the 15th. You'll be feeling more confident that a change is as good as a holiday.

You could be shocked to learn that someone whose opinion you value now expects you to take on greater responsibility. A pre-emptive strike on your part on the 18th will defuse the situation if you're brave enough to speak your mind. You know that the person has been taking liberties with you, so don't turn a blind eye. Talk to them before it's too late.

On the 24th, if you have a difference of opinion with your friend or partner over something in the past, stick to the relevant issues. The best advice I can give you is to look forward, not backwards.

Between the 23rd and the 28th, Venus's presence in your zone of travels is lucky for attracting partners, particularly those who are a little unusual and possibly at a distance. A blind date or an encounter might turn out to be very different than what you'd visualised. You may discover something endearing about this person in time, so be patient.

Work and money

Save hard for that trip or relocation, even if it means some additional sacrifices. You may be feeling the heat between the 5th and the 7th and generally up until the time you leave, so make sure you have enough dollars.

You can have a realisation, an epiphany of sorts, during this planetary phase. You may gain some insights or financial wisdom but you could have to keep this to yourself, because you'll realise that your friends aren't quite as savvy about these things as you are. 'Thinking big' is a habit that few people cultivate and this could be your problem, especially between the 16th and 21st.

Your financial impulses could be off-target on the 24th. Be careful. What you think is a good deal is likely to be anything but. Take your time and listen to the advice of those who know better.

Your desire for a fresh new lifestyle may be out of sync with what you can afford between the 27th and 30th. It is making the gap between what you have and what you don't have seem even bigger than you thought. In turn this will create more dissatisfaction. Whatever happened to slow and steady wins the race?

Destiny dates

Positive: 8, 9, 10, 11, 15, 25, 26

Negative: 22

Mixed: 3, 4, 5, 6, 7, 16, 17, 18, 19, 20, 21, 23, 24, 27, 28, 29, 30

Highlights of the month

This month's focus is on your professional activities and how you can better equip yourself to achieve the goals you have set. You must remember that success is, to a large extent, a measure of one's character and commitment to being the best they can be in any chosen field.

You will be strongly wishing that you could be doing something else, particularly if you are in a dead-end job. A commitment to stepping out of this circular life arrangement is something I recommend you seriously consider in April.

Between the 1st and 3rd, step off the spinning wheel called life and consider carefully the options before you. If you have indeed connected with the mentor I mentioned earlier in the year, your communications with that person will serve you well; but, as a Leo, sometimes you do have the tendency to believe you know best when in fact some simple humility will present to you windows of opportunity you never believed existed.

The full Moon of the 9th brings your communications full circle and good news will be received at this time. Make those important calls and set your appointments firmly in your diary, especially if they are work related.

By the 15th you may need to push a little harder to achieve your objectives. Don't let a few knock-backs deter you from achieving your objectives. You will make good headway between the 17th and the 20th, when extra attention to such things as your résumé and personal grooming will have the desired effect on interviewers and potential employers.

On the 24th and 25th you may be surprised at the arrival of a new opportunity that could suddenly arise out of nowhere. My recommendation is for you to trust your intuition and jump at whatever chance life brings you because this will be a turning point for many Leos.

You will feel well supported this month in your relationships, particularly on the material level, and your partner or closest friend will also be a great moral support. If you are married, however, it is a safer bet to discuss your proposed decisions before actually making them rather than finding that the decision you made is not at all in keeping with your partner's plans.

The key words for success in balancing your work and personal life seem to be 'general consensus'. By making sure that everyone is on the same page, you will avoid disruptions and disagreements and can enjoy sharing your success with the group.

Romance and friendship

If you sweep relationship problems under the rug, it's only a matter of time before the issues resurface. On the 1st and 2nd you may be feeling this in a few areas of your life, particularly in a close and meaningful relationship.

Systematically address your problems with anyone you have in mind, one by one, in the period up to the 8th. You'll feel like a whole new person by week's end.

You want to be seen as new, exciting and a step ahead of others, but make sure you don't do this at the expense of keeping in tune with your true self. On the 12th and 13th you'll discover that pretence is a poor substitute for truth and others will see through your ploy.

Mars and Pluto will be working powerfully and positively to give you a stronger feeling of willpower, particularly by the 20th. You must be careful not to let the intensity of your purpose conflict with another person's view. If it's on the home front, you mustn't underestimate their capacity to make life difficult for you. You might end up worse for wear, so a delicate approach is the best way to go.

Bigger is not always better; but hey, it will be a lot of fun on the 23rd. You may want to get past your limitations and do things in a lavish way simply because you've read how all those pop-psychology books keep saying 'Until you make it, fake it'. Well, yes: but if it costs more than you have that means borrowing and paying it back anyway. I think you get my drift.

After the 25th, you'll have a brilliant new plan for re-establishing your social popularity and the time will be ripe for hatching it, even if you don't quite have the initial support and encouragement you'd like on side. Choose your allies carefully.

Work and money

Too much meticulous attention to detail will bog you down between the 5th and the 8th. It will make you feel out of sorts so, if necessary, farm out the nitty-gritty stuff to someone who has nothing better to do.

You'll have to fight mental laziness by the 15th and if you do you will mysteriously stumble across some good fortune at this time. This will take study and a little ferreting out of information that will be of use to you in furthering your professional and personal ambitions. The extra dose of intellectual effort will be well worth it.

A change in your work scene around the 24th will be a welcome relief, especially if tensions have been mounting with a co-worker. Reacting and putting yourself in a tighter situation won't resolve anything so getting away and having a change of pace will be ideal.

If you're confronted by overly emotional characters in your employment sphere on the 27th, just remember that two wrongs don't make a right.

You'll feel softer and more caring towards your co-workers or employees on the 28th. Don't expect your attentions and care to be returned, however. This could make you feel unappreciated in the extreme and even angry.

Destiny dates

Positive: 3, 8, 9, 17, 18, 19, 20, 23, 24, 25, 28

Negative: 5, 8, 27

Mixed: 1, 2, 12, 13, 15

Highlights of the month

Don't let self-doubt and nervousness undermine your efforts this month. On the other hand, your confidence in certain circumstances may be way over the top and unnecessary for the situation.

On the 9th and 10th, you could find yourself in a social situation where you feel inadequate. Knowing your character, you are likely to try all that little bit harder to make an impression only to find that it backfires. Listen a little more than you speak, especially with new and different people.

From the 11th to the 15th, your romantic affairs can start to pick up considerably with the Moon making a favourable aspect to Mars on the 10th and the 11th. Passions can run high and, if you are fortunate enough to meet someone who has half a brain, you will be satisfied not only physically but mentally and emotionally as well.

Be careful of exaggerated comments by those trying to sell you goods or services around the 16th. In principle, what you'll hear will make sense, but try to get down to the practical tin-tacks of what is being offered before signing up.

Self-promotion is important this month. This is also shown by the aspect of Mercury to Jupiter, albeit a difficult one. Don't be too pushy and let history speak for itself. There's an old saying in the music industry that says 'You are only as good as your last hit' and, if you rest wholly and solely on your laurels, make sure that your past hit was sufficiently impressive to warrant others investing more time and confidence in you.

The Sun is in a prime position this month for you, Leo, and can show that, notwithstanding some of these other minor details, which apparently seem negative, it is not necessarily that way. The Sun will be blazing in the upper part of your horoscope and this indicates a month of success and endurance.

The Sun and Saturn form favourable aspects, which further indicate your ability to shoulder any additional responsibilities thrown at you. Slow, steady work with a clear goal in mind will bring you not only personal satisfaction, but financial success as well.

With Mercury's entry into the profit zone of your horoscope and the new Moon on the 24th also highlighting gains, I see the last week of May being a profitable and cash surplus phase for Leo. You will be able to put aside some of that extra cash for a rainy day and I see the month of May finishing with many Leos enjoying the benefits of their own hard work.

Romance and friendship

Games of one-upmanship may win you the battle but not the war on the 1st. You need to look at the long-term ramifications of flexing your muscles (ego). A show of humility in your love life will work better for you if you can learn to hold back.

Food choices are not particularly good for your physical health on the 3rd; this may also be impacting upon your mental and emotional clarity.

If you're sitting on the fence on the 10th, it might put you in hot water if other parties are expecting a decision from you. An easy solution to this is to make a firm decision one way or the other without playing one party off against another.

Overworking and staying up late certainly increases your work output and improves your income; however, this may not be going down too well with your nearest and dearest who are expecting you to give a little more at this time. Take some rest, clear your mind and put a bit more effort into your relationships between the 15th and 19th.

You may need to get out your little black address book and look up an old friend around the 20th because they may be able to help you with a particular problem you have. You may think you have reached a dead end but there is someone who has a solution.

There's an increased connection with foreigners in the last week of the month and making contact with them or someone at a distance is likely. You will have to set yourself some new parameters to enjoy this relationship. If the person is demanding you may need to find a compromise that sits well with both of you.

Work and money

The masculine energies in your horoscope are strong this month and this is particularly so in your workplace. You may be connecting more with the feminine side of your nature, when all the while the demands of your work are more for the aggressive and ruthless male principles. These issues could reach a pinnacle around the full Moon of the 9th and dealing with a strong male figure could be high on your agenda.

Someone may be talking behind your back around the 12th and 13th. This will require some quick and decisive action on your part to weed out who these people are and who is responsible for passing on these rumours.

With Venus in your zone of legalities this month, you can expect to have to pay extra attention to some of your contractual or workplace obligations. Through Mars there could be an obsessional aspect to the mix and, especially with Pluto's challenge, you mustn't let your decisions be coloured by any excessive passion.

Your emotional and changeable nature could work well for you if you're involved in sales, marketing or advertising, but you may be missing certain subtle points around the 24th. There could be a shake-up in your workplace around the 27th. Shooting from the hip is certainly not advisable in the last few days of May.

Destiny dates

Positive: 11, 14, 20

Negative: 1, 3, 9, 27

Mixed: 10, 12, 13, 15, 16, 17, 18, 19, 24

Highlights of the month

Your push for success continues throughout the middle part of 2009, with Mars making a dramatic impact on your profession. Mercury also having performed a retrospective move requests that you pay special attention when re-appraising your position in employment matters.

A cautionary note here is that Mars may make you a little too dominant among your peers, and even if you are asked to steer the course of your group or business temporarily, do it in a way that does not alienate others. The phrase 'quietly assertive' comes to mind.

With all this success indicated, why would it be that you are worried about money this month, I ask? These are not crushing concerns, but it does appear the conjunction of the Moon and Saturn in your earnings zone points to this fact.

The full Moon of the 7th is excellent for reconnecting you with youngsters and children generally. If you have been far too busy to give them the time you would like, set aside some moments for them now as you will both benefit by it.

If keeping up with the Jones's is something that you made a habit of, the causes of your worries will now become much clearer. Do things at your own pace without too much comparison, particularly around the 8th and 9th when you are likely to feel dissatisfied with your lot. Try to remain content with what you have and, as one of my mentors once said, to be happy—truly, deeply happy—get rid of what you haven't got.

If you are a middle-aged Leo, and your children are now in their early and mid twenties, I see this as a period of transition in which the opportunity for one or more of them to fly the coop arises. You need to be gracious about going with the flow and accepting that it is now their time to make a life for themselves. You will be busily engaged in advising them and helping to steer them in the right direction.

Venus and Mars are the archetypes of male and female energies, according to astrology. This month they are combined and in fact spend considerable time in each other's company, indicating your passion and zest for life and love will be on the increase. Because this combination occurs in your professional zone, it may herald the coming of a lover from that direction or, on a more mundane level, may simply mean an increased passion for the work you are doing.

Romance and friendship

Relationships are powerful between the 6th and 11th and also fortunate during this phase of the year. With Venus moving into passionate proximity to Mars, you'll need to pay attention, particularly to your morals and reputation.

Your attention continues to be on emotional matters and in particular the 13th and 14th shows that personal issues can come to the fore. Deeper longstanding issues need to be addressed and spoken about honestly.

With the influence of Mars passing through the upper part of your horoscope, the 18th and 19th should prove to be exciting and passionate days for you. Don't scatter your energies in ways that result in nothing socially or romantically productive.

You're very attractive and dominating in your social scene after the 22nd, but I caution you not to take centre stage at the expense of another's goodwill. You may be ignoring the fact that they're slightly envious and could feel threatened by your glamorous aura at this time.

You'll want to transform your social contacts by the 25th. An ever-widening circle is possible now, but be wise in how you use these without upsetting your current friends and social agenda.

With Jupiter continuing to transit your zone of relationships, your idealism is strong, particularly with Neptune's influence. However, by the 28th you might find some responsibilities and sacrifices requiring you to meet the needs of your partner first, even if yours haven't quite been met in the same way. But hang in there because I can assure you, you will turn the corner shortly.

Around the 30th love affairs may be on your mind, but you must not be too quick off the mark because this will be seen as a form of immaturity by the person whose attention you are seeking. Move slowly, gracefully, and you'll be more successful in your romantic flirtations at the close of June.

Work and money

Getting people to perform at the standard you are accustomed to will be extremely frustrating between the 1st and 8th. Unforeseen delays and problems, particularly associated with computers, music or other electrical equipment, mean a huge erosion of your time and an adjustment in your schedule. These difficulties may reach a peak around the 15th. Just be patient.

Fortunately your health should improve somewhat between the 18th and 22nd. You'll be feeling buoyed by the Sun shining on the horizon and your wellbeing and vitality are on the increase. With Mars moving in the upper part of your horoscope you need as much energy as you can to get through an ever-demanding workload.

Luxury, additional expenses and a pat on your own back will be in order for a job well done around the 23rd. This will be the time to celebrate and pamper yourself just a little more.

You have a strong choice to make on the 28th. You'll either be able to take some time out and kick back to enjoy the sunshine or continue to do your work and feel a little under the weather as a result. Do what needs to be done and perform today's tasks immediately.

Destiny dates

Positive: 10, 11, 15, 18, 19, 20, 21, 23, 25

Negative: 1, 2, 3, 4, 5, 6, 7, 8, 9

Mixed: 13, 14, 22, 28, 30

Highlights of the month

More energy and drive seem to be the key features of your life in July, with an added touch of sensuality thrown in to keep life interesting. Mars and Venus excite the passions and reveal that your instincts to find a suitable partner will be very strong, indeed. If you are working in a job with someone who quietly has had an eye on you, this month will be the time when thoughts and words are translated into deeds and actions. And, provocative those actions may be.

You are likely this month to be spurred on to do things you might not ordinarily do. There is an element of excitement and danger in the mix of planets for you and, if unattached, this adventure may be fulfilling if not long-lasting. However, if you are currently in a relationship, you could be tempted to venture out into a territory that can be hard to get your head around morally or ethically.

If your present relationships are rock solid, this won't present any problem and may not be a temptation at all. However, if your marriage or relationship has been on shaky ground, the temptation is real and you must now quietly assess the impact of any impulsive actions.

The key dates to note for erratic and impulsive behaviour are the 4th, 7th, and again on the 12th. Try to think through the impact of your actions on those you love before venturing forward.

Communications with a friend after the 19th are strained as they make their inquisitive nature powerfully felt. This is a time when conversations can become so deep that they border on cultural taboos. You may not want to reveal certain aspects of your personal life, but will be asked to do so as a form of loyalty. How you handle this will be an incredible test of your psychological flexibility.

While the Sun is in the quiet zone of your horoscope till the 21st or 22nd, you will probably prefer to lay low and not have too much to do with your usual group of friends or family. I do recommend that if you have a preference to hold things close to your chest, do so. You must not feel obliged to reveal everything to everyone because this then places you in a vulnerable position.

Home matters are favoured due to the lunar position this month. Favourable influences from several planets mean that you can tie up loose ends with family and relatives. Cousins or other family members you haven't heard from in a while will cheer you up, but may also erode your time due to a sense of obligation to meeting their needs.

Romance and friendship

Between the 3rd and 5th, don't let confusion dominate your emotional landscape. If there are issues with your relationships, look at the facts and only the facts and try as hard as you can to leave your feelings out of the picture. Your decisions will then be absolutely correct.

If on the 7th you feel like a doormat in respect to some friend, who are you going to blame? You're the one allowing yourself to be trodden all over. Stand up, assert your rights, and you'll feel much better for it.

A fine period for reconnecting with friends and long-lost partners occurs between the 8th and 14th. In particular the 16th is a day when you can re-establish a romance that some time ago had come to a grinding halt. Communication through a third party, perhaps a mutual friend, will help kick-start this relationship again.

Social affairs are strong between the 18th and 19th but you might find yourself in a somewhat dreamy state around the 20th and 21st, so keep your wits about you. If you daydream too much you could find yourself lagging behind your friends and being completely out of step.

There's an excellent omen for some personal breakthrough around the 23rd. Communicate your creative ideas to those who understand where you're coming from. If you bite your tongue you'll be shutting yourself off from an important gateway to social success.

A personal favour owed to you needs to be repaid. You'll be treading on eggshells around the 28th, worrying about hurting the other person's feelings or perhaps ruining a relationship. You should ask them about this matter. Perhaps you have loaned them money, which you shouldn't have done in the first place, and the only way to approach it is with a businesslike manner.

Work and money

On the 7th and 8th you can expect many calls, and nuisance ones at that. Hopefully you have an assistant to help you get through the pile of work that is outstanding. Make sure you have a good work schedule and plan your manoeuvres before each day begins.

Your personal prowess is at a strong point around the 15th, even though you may have been feeling a little low key during the Sun's quiet transit of your twelfth zone of privacy. This will put you in a strong position if you are an employer because you'll be looking to bring in new people, fresh new blood, to inject into your projects.

Thoroughly check the credentials of those you interview and don't take things for granted. On the 22nd you might overlook an important detail that may seem only minor at first.

You'll have to question the amount of work being thrown your way on the 29th. It isn't being distributed evenly among the group, wouldn't you agree? Who's the person in charge? Is there anyone calling the shots? You need to stand up, speak your mind and make sure you're not doing an unfair share of the work.

Destiny dates

Positive: 9, 10, 11, 13, 14, 15, 16, 18, 23

Negative: 3, 4, 5, 29

Mixed: 7, 8, 12, 19, 20, 21, 22, 28

Highlights of the month

It is a lucky month for you, Leo, as the Moon activates the speculative zone of your horoscope. You may attempt a punt or some risky financial activity, which, although going against your better judgement and frugal ways of late, may prove to pay off rather handsomely. Coupled with Mars's presence in your profit zone, this should highlight a period of intense activity and improvement in your financial affairs.

Some Leos may develop a taste for speculation in local and foreign stock markets. Remember, all stock trading is a form of gambling, but there are ways to minimise that through careful analysis and education. I recommend that you investigate these avenues more thoroughly to gain the best return on your money.

This is also a creative month for you and you can feel inspired by friends who are actively engaged in activities that are now drawing your attention. The music, arts and other craft-related activities could be something through which you find a satisfactory emotional outlet. This is also pertinent due to the fact that the passionate Venus and Mars are now separating in the heavens, leaving you free to pursue what you feel is your own personal need.

In the coming weeks, particularly after the 16th, you will be more prone to lavish some of your well-earned money on yourself. Spending money on beautifying your home, purchasing materials for creating those wonderful Leo works of art (which will eventually have your signature on them), will be an enjoyable way to spend your money.

Don't let boredom set in this month. Enrol in an evening class where you can put your talents to good use and where you will also be surprised to meet others of like-minds. I see a new social peer group arising and this is an excellent time in which to forge new friendships and to expand your horizons mentally, too.

Your health is quite strong this month, with the Sun returning to its birth place of Leo. Generally, however, because of uplifting energy and confidence, it is also possible that you will want to do much more than you usually do with this surplus life force.

Pick your activities wisely and screen people for their motivations because you can ill afford to do everything.

Health issues are likely to arise through overwork and/or spreading yourself too thinly. But with a higher level of vitality comes a desire to do sport, too, so do take care to not overdo it, particularly around the 28th and 29th.

Romance and friendship

Investigate new opportunities to take your relationship to a higher level between the 4th and 6th. It will bring renewed social opportunities, improved personal skills and a closeness with your partner.

Don't let that aimless or confused state drag you down on the 12th. How do you want the world to perceive you? Think outside the square, dare to think differently and by the 15th you'll hit upon something quite novel and fulfilling.

It's best to avoid any confrontation around the 16th, even if you feel that what you have to say is correct. You mustn't operate from a base of ego, especially up to the 20th. Foster peace, not war.

If you find yourself in a position where the discussion is completely outside your own interests on the 23rd, go beyond the superficialities of the topic to the motivation behind what is being said. You'll handle the meeting or gathering with a much better state of mind.

Intimacy may not flow quite so well around the 27th and 28th and, if you're feeling that your partner is unemotional or unresponsive, you'll have to put in some extra effort to get them to a more affectionate state of mind.

On the 30th your talent for excellent speech can be put to good use, particularly if you're interested in someone new on the block. This is a lucky period where your words will have maximum impact and the responses you get from that special person will be just what you're looking for.

Perfecting your technique in the bedroom will be a key issue for you in the last few days of the month. If you become too much of a perfectionist, however, you'll find yourself missing the art of spontaneity and this is of course 90 per cent of the fun of it.

Work and money

Fixing your friendships with work colleagues is ideal around the 2nd and 3rd. Take the time to bridge the gap between your life and the life of your co-workers, especially if you feel you've been a little distant and disconnected from them lately.

By the 12th you'll be prepared to take a gamble on that lifestyle issue and move in a direction that sometime ago would have scared the living daylights out of you. You'll have the courage to make your dreams come true.

You don't necessarily have to work as hard as you thought to achieve some of the successes you have quietly dreamed about. The new Moon on the 20th brings together your enthusiasm and cheerful generosity to help you win a new friend or ally who will be instrumental in your future success.

You'll make some breakthroughs in delegating parts of your work overload to others around the 28th and 29th. Maximise your time by using their talents to help you achieve your goals. This is an important element in your life throughout the coming period. Simply put, it means you'll have some free time at your disposal and this could make you feel a lot more relaxed.

Destiny dates

Positive: 2, 3, 4, 5, 6, 30

Negative: Nil

Mixed: 12, 20, 23, 27, 28, 29

Highlights of the month

Venus occupies one of the finest positions in the zodiac for Leo this month. In its proximity to your birth Sun, your grace and attractiveness will reach new heights.

On the 2nd and 3rd you will be inspired to create a new persona. Consequently, you may shop till you drop, looking for that new outfit or fashion statement that will now help you make your mark upon the world.

I also have the sense that your desire to go up-market in fashions could hold an influence on your physique; such things as hairstyling, manicuring and, possibly even in the extreme, cosmetic surgery to that feature that has bothered you over the years. If this is something that has affected your self-esteem at the deepest level, by all means make the changes.

However, if this is a feeble attempt on your part to lift your self-confidence from the outside in, you may feel few rewards at the end of the process. My strong recommendation is that you talk to your GP and get the psychological thumbs up before making any permanent change to your face or your body.

Diet will also be important this month, as shown by the position of the Sun in the zone of eating and culinary delights. With its association with Saturn, particularly from the Moon of the 18th, you may make some new resolutions by which you can remodel your physique with disciplining the intake of food and the output of energy, as in sport and exercise. Incorporating these two aspects will yield Leos a fine result in the last part of 2009.

With the association of the Sun and Saturn, I can safely predict a fairly strong period of responsibility and a growing workload. If you spend adequate time working through your diary and getting a neat and orderly timetable in place, this period will work wonderfully well for you in helping you move to the next level of success.

On the 25th and 26th, the power of the Sun, Saturn, the Moon and Pluto will drive this point home. If you are ill-prepared for some new project or a change of direction in your company for personal independent business, you may be putting in far more hours than you would like to, hence the added importance of health and dietary management this month.

The full Moon, which occurs earlier in the month, comes to fruition around the 30th, with shared resources, wills, legacies and such things as insurances and taxes taking the limelight. On top of your already intense workload, you may be a little bothered to have to attend to these matters, but it is not a bad idea to do so.

Romance and friendship

If you judge another person's eager statements as a form of aggression you'll miss the point of your communication on the 3rd. Try not to judge others based upon your own personality and standards and maintain an open mind.

Don't let confusion regarding friends and their intentions bother you around the 9th. Suspicion will prevail but I suggest you simply ask the appropriate questions. It may not be the answer you want but it will be the truth.

You may have burned a few bridges with someone who's able to get you out of a relationship pickle around the 12th. You'll have to eat some humble pie to get them back on side and move you through to the next level of this issue.

Between the 14th and 16th, demonstrations of passion by a member of the opposite sex will be unwanted as your view of the friendship will be very different. Unfortunately you may have inadvertently given off the wrong signals and now you'll have to backtrack to set the record straight.

A social event or invitation on the 19th may be associated with your professional activities and is very likely to introduce a whole different way of thinking and a new set of friends.

You could have some feisty banter with friends after the 24th. You may be surprised to see a side of someone's nature you hadn't thought possible but don't take the situation too seriously or let this sever the bonds of your friendship.

You mustn't let your technical or worldly knowledge limit you in the area of your relationships after the 29th. Learn to accept your limitation and be honest about your own level of knowledge. This will gain you a great deal of respect.

Work and money

If you're too busy worrying about what's in it for you on the 4th, you'll be doing yourself a long-term disservice. Remember the laws of karma are simple, even when it comes to making money and fostering your own professional opportunities. Even if you don't have what you perceive as the time to help someone, by doing it, magic does happen.

Coming across incidental items is not going to make you rich, you realise that, don't you? Affording yourself a few little luxuries between the 10th and 12th is necessary so stop feeling guilty about the fact that you are doing it.

As your popularity increases so too will your chance of improving your income, but you may inwardly feel a slight doubt about your ability to lead people at their level, on your terms. Between the 19th and 25th, take the time to work at a little self-education in terms of your job, skill sets and your character.

You'll have to get into the way things are moving after the 26th. Your mind may be closed to some issue such as utilising the Internet as a means of networking your product and services. You must take the time to familiarise yourself with new forms of communication and knowledge.

Destiny dates

Positive: 2, 3, 10, 11, 19, 20, 21, 22, 23, 24, 25, 26, 30

Negative: 9

Mixed: 3, 4, 12, 14, 15, 16, 29

Highlights of the month

You can feel a little ineffectual, but not because you are unable to manage your duties this month, but because Mars occupies the water sign of Cancer and is in the low key portion of your horoscope. This position of Mars may have been felt in September as well. You must listen to your body's signals and not push yourself beyond your limits, which nature tells you will cause you harm.

An excess workload is part of the problem, as I see it, so this means curtailing some of your other activities to create some space, a simple but necessary procedure in October.

Between the 3rd and the 7th your attention will be on work matters. I should rephrase that and say your activities will be centred on work matters but your attention will be far from connected to them. You may want to be anywhere but working, which is understandable given the current pattern of energies for you.

Venus, Mercury and Saturn are combined in the area of finances and give an aesthetic twist to this practical department of your life. This is an opportunity for you to consider how money can be made through antiques, artefacts and other not-so-ordinary techniques. This is also a literary combination, which shows that you are more interested in losing yourself in a good book rather than physically getting among the world. Again, trust your inner voice.

By the new Moon of the 18th your mind will be stimulated to re-engage with friends and family. Along with the Sun traversing this area of your life, you can expect an upswing in communication.

Contracts and other forms of agreements will be high on your agenda and this is a favourable period in which to secure a deal in written form or simply by a handshake. Be careful, though, because Jupiter, the Moon and Neptune point to the fact that clarity could become a little blurred if either party hasn't diligently combed through the fine print of any agreement. It is always a good idea, especially if friends or family are involved, to define clearly the terms and any exit strategies that may be necessary.

Speaking of partnerships, business is of course not the only type of association that comes under these astrological categories. After the 25th, the consummation of a long-term relationship may be genuinely possible with marriage and other long-term romantic commitments being favoured. As with my previous statements this month, make sure you understand the terms and conditions before committing yourself emotionally.

Romance and friendship

Don't be too pushy in going for what you want, particularly in the second half of the month. Understatement and a more relaxed attitude is likely to win you favour with someone who matters on the 8th. A new relationship you've been waiting for is about to enter your life if you're single and unattached.

If you're currently in a relationship you can expect a huge improvement in it during the period of the 12th to the 16th.

You need to bury the hatchet over something you've both held a grudge about and move forward.

Take the time to spend a little extra money beautifying yourself and looking the part on the 20th. First impressions do count and, although you may feel that you could save a little money by wearing an existing outfit, it won't take you to the level that is now possible. Spend a little more freely.

Avoid any confrontation on the 24th, particularly later in the day. Friends and relatives on the home front could make waves so maintaining a quiet, low-key profile is the better option. By the 25th your relationships will be more passionate and interesting.

Your mind will be quick and agile on the 29th and this is typical of your personality. Several opportunities will arise for travel and meeting new people. If romance gets off to a shaky start, rest assured it will be much more satisfying, especially if you make that extra effort.

A tendency to be erratic with your feelings needs to be checked around the 30th. Saying one thing and doing another will put you on shaky ground. Make sure your agreements of an emotional nature are airtight and don't accept something the other person says for the sake of pleasing them. All parties have to be satisfied with the outcome for the long-term.

Work and money

Your physical wellbeing will be essential to maintain your optimum energy levels around the 10th. With Mars in the quiet zone of your horoscope, lack of sleep, poor diet and any emotional confusion will start to catch up on you.

Any sudden lunge at a new job may be based on the wrong premise on the 15th and I advise you to think carefully before jumping out of the pan and into the fire. Someone you meet could give you an exciting new perspective on life, but don't expect that to be the panacea for all your professional ills.

A quieter period from the 18th to the 23rd needs to be accepted gracefully. If you're not feeling particularly motivated you should use this time productively in other ways because your frustration won't help your cause. Social events also associated with your work are not all they're cracked up to be. Don't invest a lot of time in something that will give you little in return.

Make some extra time on your calendar on the 26th as you'll be inundated with unexpected demands from everyone around you. A workplace romance is in the air on the 29th and 30th but try not to take on too much.

Destiny dates

Positive: 8, 10, 12, 13, 14, 16, 18, 19, 20, 22, 23, 25, 29

Negative: 24

Mixed: 3, 4, 5, 6, 7, 15, 26, 30

Highlights of the month

Mars shakes you up, wakes you from your lethargy and prepares you for an active and productive month in November. With the influence of Jupiter, your thinking is big and bright, so I say go for your dreams. However, while that might seem easy at first, on the 8th you may be opposed by your nearest and dearest.

You have to exercise diplomacy in answering their questions and, especially if you are married or in a de facto relationship, the questions about how, when and why you need to spend money will be irritating, but necessary.

Try not to be wasteful this month and the key word is consultation in any of your financial dealings. Mercury, the Sun and Venus hint at the fact you will be keen to sign up for the 'Two year, interest free, no deposit packages' at one of the local malls.

You will realise this is false economising, especially because there's no way you will have that money two years down the track. It could be that your partner is not too far off the mark in saying that your dreams, as big and lavish as they are, may not be practical just now. Talk about your ambitions and how you are going to afford and make payments for your ideas.

You have a warm and affable nature this month and generally feel optimistic and generous in your friendships. There is a strong tie-in with your peer group, best friends and your home life as well. It is likely you will entertain at home and want to make this the pivot of your social activities.

You will be interested in taking up an unexpected offer of love sometime after the 13th. Someone off-beat or with a different approach to life can sweep you off your feet if you are not careful. Venus indicates artists, smooth-talkers and people from foreign cultures or at least fringe-dwellers of our own society.

I see many novel interactions and episodes possible due to this astrological combination, but don't expect too much of a future with any new character unless you are prepared to make significant adjustments to your lifestyle.

The new Moon on the 16th indicates a shift away from your current living circumstances and suggests that you may want a radical overhaul in terms of where you live.

This also reflects changes in your relationship with your mother or other females in your family. Understanding your roots and gaining additional insights into your family tradition is quite possible.

In the later part of the month, some Leos might opt to take an early Christmas break or long service leave.

Romance and friendship

Being overly generous will get you into hot water as others may misinterpret your demonstrations of love on the 8th. They may think you have some sort of ulterior motive. Pick your mark and choose your time wisely if you do genuinely want to help someone. You could on the other hand be the recipient of a gift very soon.

Relationships will be high on the agenda between the 13th and 18th, but you may have to make a choice between the lesser of two evils. You will in the end have an insight like a bolt out of the blue, which will make your choice clear and certain.

You can try fighting for what you believe in on the 24th, but don't forget that compromise is also good. Get in there and get what you want and your firm stance will actually win over your partner.

You could be interested in sports and other competitive activities between the 18th and the 25th. Your friends will now be behind you 100 per cent in your choices.

By the 28th you'll be keen to work out the details of your future. The important thing is not to leave things half finished. You'll get a bright green light on a project or a bureaucratic challenge will be cleared up, leaving time for more pleasurable activities.

Beware of the intentions of others on the 29th when you could be a little more gullible than usual. You may have forewarning of the situation by a close friend who has information you don't. Be receptive to their suggestions and good advice as they have nothing to gain from steering you in the wrong direction.

On the 30th, have a quiet night at home entertaining a friend or lover. Set the mood with some candlelight and soft music and let your mind dwell on the sentimental and nostalgic aspects of life. This will be a beautiful end to the month.

Work and money

Mars makes you bold and beautiful throughout November but be careful that your certainty on different matters around the 1st and 2nd are not met with opposition. Wait until the 3rd when Venus and Neptune track favourable communication circumstances and the deal you've been waiting to push through will have a better chance of success.

Property matters after the 8th go well, with Venus creating profitable circumstances in any investments related to land and housing. Make sure that if you're selling a property, the advertising and the costs associated with it are clarified with the agent beforehand.

Brilliant ideas can be shared around the 11th with Mercury and Uranus making your ideas popular. If you're looking for an investor for one of your ideas, things should be clearer by the 22nd.

Work may be a little dull around the 25th to the 30th but you'll still be able to make slow but steady progress. Don't rush things as you may have to make corrections for the sake of saving time.

Destiny dates

Positive: 3, 8, 11, 19, 20, 21, 22, 23, 24

Negative: 8, 26, 27, 29

Mixed: 1, 2, 13, 14, 15, 16, 17, 18, 25, 28, 30

Highlights of the month

I see that you are able to sustain the high level of energy and drive that I mentioned in November due to Mars's continued presence in your Sun sign. I'm cautioning you to restrain your impulses, particularly of a physical nature, because you are likely to be speedy, overactive and accident prone as well.

If you are driving and travelling to meet deadlines, remember the last month of the year is usually more hectic than others due to the Christmas rush. Make allowances for this and give yourself extra time to arrive at your destinations safely.

Mars and Jupiter oppose each other this month, so you must continue your dialogue with your partner to make sure your philosophies are in harmony with each other. This is of primary importance because I mentioned in the outset of the yearly forecast that this is one of the most notable relationship cycles in twelve years. You don't want to blow it, Leo! Just because you have a prime opportunity does not mean you will make a better reality. All relationships require hard work and in this last phase of 2009 you must not let your attention to detail slip.

Gestures of love and affection on the new Moon of the 16th will go a long way to smoothing over any tensions you have, and this being the week before Christmas will help consider-ably in making the Christmas get-together all that more enjoyable.

Your commitments take backstage even though you are probably a little emotional about what is required and at the end of the day you may have to leave off some unfinished business to the new year. Don't worry yourself over this and ruin your Christmas break because these are minor duties that can wait.

Love reaches a pinnacle around the 19th when mutual affections can make you feel that this year has been well worth the efforts you have made. Venus also accompanies the Sun in the fifth zone of love and creative satisfaction.

I see this as a rounding-off of the year with a lot of personal satisfaction and love. Family members will reciproc-ate and offer you the support you have wished for and this can be the start of a whole new dynamic in your family life.

Saturn also is now entering an important two-and-a-half-year phase and signifies that your financial struggles should be coming to an end. This could be an easier period in which you will earn well and in which your debts can now be paid off.

This suggests that you can enter the new year refreshed, relaxed and with a more optimistic view of your capacity to save and acquire the lifestyle you so desire.

This has been an exciting year and one in which the chal-lenges have edged you closer to a deeper level of spiritual and emotional fulfilment. I trust that this pattern will continue into 2010 with the stars shining upon you more brightly, Leo. Good luck with the coming period.

Romance and friendship

Be consistent with your words this month as much is resting upon it. On the 1st, 2nd and the 7th, you'll be asked to explain yourself and, even though a slip-up on your part may have been innocent, you'll be crucified for it.

Love is hot around the 14th with Venus, Mercury and the Sun activating your romance and love life. The new Moon on the 16th is excellent for establishing a new relationship and affairs of the young and children will also bring a great deal of satisfaction.

The week or so leading up to Christmas is full of wonderful aspects and, on the 15th, Jupiter in fine aspect to the Sun brings with it the promise of exciting possibilities in your love life. A promise, a token or gift is unexpected but warmly received.

Venus and Jupiter on the 21st show that you'll be lavishing your love and attention on friends and family alike this year. Don't go overboard in feeling that you must purchase expensive gifts, however, as it is the thought that counts.

By the 28th the conjunction of Venus and Pluto will bring out the obsessive quality of your love or that of another. Don't smother or scare away a potential suitor through any insecurity that the relationship may not last. A more relaxed approach has a far better chance of attracting and keeping a lover close to you.

It's best to spend time alone between the 29th and 31st because this will give you the chance to think carefully about who that secret admirer may be. If you've received a gift from a stranger or someone you're not sure about, it's likely that the person in question is actually more familiar with you than you think.

Work and money

December is always a time when the dates on your calendar will appear a lot closer than they are. Time constraints, what appear to be heavier deadlines and greater demands are likely, especially between the 6th and the 8th.

You can't sit back and rest on your past achievements because you know that unfinished business is sitting in your in-tray and will only cause you worry over the Christmas break. Work a little bit harder up until the 17th so you can enjoy the Christmas break.

Inspiration is strong by the 20th with the continued association of Neptune and Jupiter in your zone of partnerships. This is a mutually beneficial period for learning and teaching equally. Some of your studies will pay off now and give you a sense of real accomplishment.

This is also a month in which some special accolades can be received, if not a promise of a new position with greater responsibility and higher pay.

Christmas and the day after will be a time of great celebration this year and part of that will be the successes that will become evident right up until the 11th hour in 2009.

Destiny dates

Positive: 14, 15, 16, 19, 20, 21, 25

Negative: 6, 8

Mixed: 1, 2, 7, 17, 28, 29, 30, 31

2009:
Astronumerology

A failure is a man who has blundered, but is not able to cash in on the experience.

—Elbert Hubbard

The power behind your name

By adding the numbers of your name you can see which planet is ruling you. Each of the letters of the alphabet is assigned a number, which is tabled below. These numbers are ruled by the planets. This is according to the ancient Chaldean system of numerology and is very different to the Pythagorean system to which many refer.

Each number is assigned a planet:

AIQJY	=	1	**Sun**
BKR	=	2	**Moon**
CGLS	=	3	**Jupiter**
DMT	=	4	**Uranus**
EHNX	=	5	**Mercury**
UVW	=	6	**Venus**
OZ	=	7	**Neptune**
FP	=	8	**Saturn**
—	=	9	**Mars**

Notice that the number 9 is not allotted a letter because it is considered special. Once the numbers have been added you will see that a single planet rules your name and personal affairs. Many famous actors, writers and musicians change their names to attract the energy of a luckier planet. You can experiment with the table and try new names or add letters of your second name to see how that vibration suits you. It's a lot of fun!

Here is an example of how to find out the power of your name. If your name is John Smith, calculate the ruling planet by correlating each letter to a number in the table like this:

J O H N   S M I T H

1 7 5 5   3 4 1 4 5

Now add the numbers like this:

$1 + 7 + 5 + 5 + 3 + 4 + 1 + 4 + 5 = 35$

Then add $3 + 5 = 8$

The ruling number of John Smith's name is 8, which is ruled by Saturn. Now study the name-number table to reveal the power of your name. The numbers 3 and 5 will also play a secondary role in John's character and destiny so in this case you would also study the effects of Jupiter and Mercury.

Name-number table

Your name number	Ruling planet	Your name characteristics
1	Sun	Charismatic personality. Great vitality and life force. Physically active and outgoing. Attracts good friends and individuals in powerful positions. Good government connections. Intelligent, dramatic, showy and successful. A loyal number for relationships.
2	Moon	Soft, emotional temperament. Changeable moods but psychic, intuitive senses. Imaginative nature and compassionate expression of feelings. Loves family, mother and home life. Night owl who probably needs more sleep.

Success with the public and/or the opposite sex.

3	Jupiter	Outgoing, optimistic number with lucky overtones. Attracts opportunities without trying. Good sense of timing. Religious or spiritual aspirations. Can investigate the meaning of life. Loves to travel and explore the world and people.
4	Uranus	Explosive personality with many quirky aspects. Likes the untried and untested. Forward thinking, with many unusual friends. Gets bored easily so needs plenty of stimulating experiences. Innovative, technological and creative. Wilful and stubborn when wants to be. Unexpected events in life may be positive or negative.
5	Mercury	Quick-thinking mind with great powers of speech. Extremely active life; always on the go and lives on nervous energy. Youthful attitude and never grows old. Looks younger than actual age. Young friends and humorous disposition. Loves reading and writing.
6	Venus	Charming personality. Graceful and attractive character, who cherishes friends and social life. Musical or artistic interests. Good for money making as well as numerous love affairs. Career in

the public eye is possible. Loves family but is often overly concerned by friends.

7	Neptune	Intuitive, spiritual and self-sacrificing nature. Easily duped by those who need help. Loves to dream of life's possibilities. Has healing powers. Dreams are revealing and prophetic. Loves the water and will have many journeys in life. Spiritual aspirations dominate worldly desires.
8	Saturn	Hard-working, focused individual with slow but certain success. Incredible concentration and self-sacrifice for a goal. Money orientated but generous when trust is gained. Professional but may be a hard taskmaster. Demands highest standards and needs to learn to enjoy life a little more.
9	Mars	Incredible physical drive and ambition. Sports and outdoor activities are keys to health. Combative and likes to work and play just as hard. Protective of family, friends and territory. Individual tastes in life but is also self-absorbed. Needs to listen to others' advice to gain greater success.

Your 2009 planetary ruler

Astrology and numerology are closely linked. Each planet rules over a number between 1 and 9. Both your name and your birth date are ruled by planetary energies. Here are the planets and their ruling numbers:

1 Sun; 2 Moon; 3 Jupiter; 4 Uranus; 5 Mercury; 6 Venus; 7 Neptune; 8 Saturn; 9 Mars

Simply add the numbers of your birth date and the year in question to find out which planet will control the coming year for you. Here is an example:

If you were born on 12 November, add the numerals 1 and 2 (12, your day of birth) and 1 and 1 (11, your month of birth) to the year in question, in this case 2009 (current year), like this:

Add $1 + 2 + 1 + 1 + 2 + 0 + 0 + 9 = 16$

Then add these numbers again: $1 + 6 = 7$

The planet ruling your individual karma for 2009 will be Neptune because this planet rules the number 7.

You can even take your ruling name number as shown on page 113 and add it to the year in question to throw more light on your coming personal affairs like this:

John Smith = 8

Year coming = 2009

Add $8 + 2 + 0 + 0 + 9 = 19$

Add $1 + 9 = 10$

Add $1 + 0 = 1$

This is the ruling year number using your name number as a basis. Therefore, study the Sun's (number 1) influence for 2009. Enjoy!

1 = Year of the Sun

Overview

The Sun is the brightest object in the heavens and rules number 1 and the sign of Leo. Because of this the coming year will bring you great success and popularity.

You'll be full of life and radiant vibrations and are more than ready to tackle your new nine-year cycle, which begins now. Any new projects you commence are likely to be successful.

Your health and vitality will be very strong and your stamina at its peak. Even if you happen to have the odd problem with your health, your recuperative power will be strong.

You have tremendous magnetism this year so social popularity won't be a problem for you. I see many new friends and lovers coming into your life. Expect loads of invitations to parties and fun-filled outings. Just don't take your health for granted as you're likely to burn the candle at both ends.

With success coming your way, don't let it go to your head. You must maintain humility, which will make you even more popular in the coming year.

Love and pleasure

This is an important cycle for renewing your love and connections with your family, particularly if you have children. The Sun is connected with the sign of Leo and therefore brings an increase in musical and theatrical activities. Entertainment and other creative hobbies will be high on your agenda and bring you a great sense of satisfaction.

Work

You won't have to make too much effort to be successful this year as the brightness of the Sun will draw opportunities to you. Changes in work are likely and if you have been concerned that opportunities are few and far between, 2009 will be differ-ent. You can expect some sort of promotion or an increase in income because your employers will take special note of your skills and service orientation.

Improving your luck

Leo is the ruler of number 1 and therefore, if you're born under this star sign, 2009 will be particularly lucky. For others, July and August, the months of Leo, will bring good fortune. The 1st, 8th, 15th and 22nd hours of Sundays especially will give you a unique sort of luck in any sort of competition or activi-ties generally. Keep your eye out for those born under Leo as they may be able to contribute something to your life and may even have a karmic connection to you. This is a particularly important year for your destiny.

Your lucky numbers in this coming cycle are 1, 10, 19 and 28.

2 = Year of the Moon

Overview

There's nothing more soothing than the cool light of the full Moon on a clear night. The Moon is emotional and receptive and controls your destiny in 2009. If you're able to use the positive energies of the Moon, it will be a great year in which you can realign and improve your relationships, particularly with family members.

Making a commitment to becoming a better person and bringing your emotions under control will also dominate your thinking. Try not to let your emotions get the better of you throughout the coming year because you may be drawn into the changeable nature of these lunar vibrations as well. If you fail to keep control of your emotional life you'll later regret some of your actions. You must carefully blend thinking with feeling to arrive at the best results. Your luck throughout 2009 will certainly be determined by the state of your mind.

Because the Moon and the sign of Cancer rule the number 2 there is a certain amount of change to be expected this year. Keep your feelings steady and don't let your heart rule your head.

Love and pleasure

Your primary concern in 2009 will be your home and family life. You'll be keen to finally take on those renovations, or work on your garden. You may even think of buying a new home. You can at last carry out some of those plans and make your dreams come true. If you find yourself a little more temperamental than usual, do some extra meditation and spend time alone until you sort this out. You mustn't withhold your feelings from your partner as this will only create frustration.

Work

During 2009 your focus will be primarily on feelings and family; however, this doesn't mean you can't make great strides in your work as well. The Moon rules the general public and what you might find is that special opportunities and connections with the world at large present themselves to you. You could be working with large numbers of people.

If you're looking for a better work opportunity, try to focus your attention on women who can give you a hand. Use your intuition as it will be finely tuned this year. Work and career success depends upon your instincts.

Improving your luck

The sign of Cancer is your ruler this year and because the Moon rules Mondays, both this day of the week and the month of July are extremely lucky for you. The 1st, 8th, 15th and 22nd hours on Mondays will be very powerful. Pay special attention to the new and full Moon days throughout 2009.

The numbers 2, 11 and 29 are lucky for you.

3 = Year of Jupiter

Overview

The year 2009 will be a 3 year for you and, because of this, Jupiter and Sagittarius will dominate your affairs. This is very lucky and shows that you'll be motivated to broaden your horizons, gain more money and become extremely popular in your social circles. It looks like 2009 will be a fun-filled year with much excitement.

Jupiter and Sagittarius are generous to a fault and so likewise, your open-handedness will mark the year. You'll be friendly and helpful to all of those around you.

Pisces is also under the rulership of the number 3 and this brings out your spiritual and compassionate nature. You'll become a much better person, reducing your negative karma by increasing your self-awareness and spiritual feelings. You will want to share your luck with those you love.

Love and pleasure

Travel and seeking new adventures will be part and parcel of your romantic life this year. Travelling to distant lands and meeting unusual people will open your heart to fresh possibilities of romance.

You'll try novel and audacious things and will find yourself in a different circle of friends. Compromise will be important in making your existing relationships work. Talk about your feelings. If you are currently in a relationship you'll feel an upswing in your affection for your partner. This is a perfect opportunity to deepen your love for each other and take your relationship to a new level.

If you're not attached to someone just yet, there's good news for you. Great opportunities lie in store for you and a spiritual or karmic connection may be experienced in 2009.

Work

Great fortune can be expected through your working life in the next twelve months. Your friends and work colleagues will want to help you achieve your goals. Even your employers will be amenable to your requests for extra money or a better position within the organisation.

If you want to start a new job or possibly begin an independent line of business this is a great year to do it. Jupiter looks set to give you plenty of opportunities, success and a superior reputation.

Improving your luck

As long as you can keep a balanced view of things and not overdo anything, your luck will increase dramatically throughout 2009. The important thing is to remain grounded and not be too airy-fairy about your objectives. Be realistic about your talents and capabilities and don't brag about your skills or achievements. This will only invite envy from others.

Moderate your social life as well and don't drink or eat too much as this will slow your reflexes and lessen your chances for success.

You have plenty of spiritual insights this year so you should use them to their maximum. In the 1st, 8th, 15th and 24th hours of Thursdays you should use your intuition to enhance your luck, and the numbers 3, 12, 21 and 30 are also lucky for you. March and December are your lucky months but generally the whole year should go pretty smoothly for you.

4 = Year of Uranus

Overview

The electric and exciting planet of the zodiac Uranus and its sign of Aquarius rule your affairs throughout 2009. Dramatic events will surprise and at the same time unnerve you in your professional and personal life. So be prepared!

You'll be able to achieve many things this year and your dreams are likely to come true, but you mustn't be distracted or scattered with your energies. You'll be breaking through your own self-limitations and this will present challenges from your family and friends. You'll want to be independent and develop your spiritual powers and nothing will stop you.

Try to maintain discipline and an orderly lifestyle so you can make the most of these special energies this year. If unexpected things do happen, it's not a bad idea to have an alternative plan so you don't lose momentum.

Love and pleasure

You want something radical, something different in your relationships this year. It's quite likely that your love life will be feeling a little less than exciting so you'll take some important steps to change that. If your partner is as progressive as you'll be this year, then your relationship is likely to improve and fulfil both of you.

In your social life you will meet some very unusual people whom you'll feel are specially connected to you spiritually. You may want to ditch everything for the excitement and passion of a completely new relationship, but tread carefully as this may not work out exactly as you'd expected.

Work

Technology, computing and the Internet will play a larger role in your professional life this coming year. You'll have to move ahead with the times and learn new skills if you want to achieve success.

A hectic schedule is likely, so make sure your diary is with you at all times. Try to be more efficient and don't waste time.

New friends and alliances at work will help you achieve even greater success in the coming period. Becoming a team player will be even more important towards gaining satisfaction in your professional endeavours.

Improving your luck

Moving too quickly and impulsively will cause you problems on all fronts, so be a little more patient and think your decisions through more carefully. Social, romantic and professional opportunities will come to you but take a little time to investigate the ramifications of your actions.

The 1st, 8th, 15th and 20th hours of any Saturday are lucky, but love and luck are likely to cross your path when you least expect it. The numbers 4, 13, 22 and 31 are also lucky for you this year.

5 = Year of Mercury

Overview

The supreme planet of communication, Mercury, is your ruling planet throughout 2009. The number 5, which is connected to Mercury, will confer upon you success through your intellectual abilities.

Any form of writing or speaking will be improved and this will be, to a large extent, underpinning your success. Your imagination will be stimulated by this planet with many incredible new and exciting ideas coming to mind.

Mercury and the number 5 are considered somewhat indecisive. Be firm in your attitude and don't let too many ideas or opportunities distract and confuse you. By all means get as much information as you can to help you make the right decision.

I see you involved with money proposals, job applications, even contracts that need to be signed so remain clear-headed as much as possible.

Your business skills and clear and concise communication will be at the heart of your life in 2009.

Love and pleasure

Mercury, which rules the signs of Gemini and Virgo, will make your love life a little difficult due to its changeable nature. On the one hand you'll feel passionate and loving to your partner, yet on the other you will feel like giving it all up for the excitement of a new affair. Maintain the middle ground.

Also, try not to be too critical with your friends and family members. The influence of Virgo makes you prone to expecting much more from others than they're capable of giving. Control your sharp tongue and don't hurt people's feelings. Encouraging others is the better path, leading to more emotional satisfaction.

Work

Speed will dominate your professional life in 2009. You'll be flitting from one subject to another and taking on far more than you can handle. You'll need to make some serious changes in your routine to handle the avalanche of work that will come your way. You'll also be travelling with your work, but not necessarily overseas.

If you're in a job you enjoy then this year will give you additional successes. If not, it may be time to move on.

Improving your luck

Communication is the secret of attaining your desires in the coming twelve months. Keep focused on one idea rather than scattering your energies in all directions and your success will be speedier.

By looking after your health, sleeping well and exercising

regularly, you'll build up your resilience and mental strength.

The 1st, 8th, 15th and 20th hours of Wednesday are lucky so it's best to schedule your meetings and other important social engagements during these times. The lucky numbers for Mercury are 5, 14, 23 and 32.

6 = Year of Venus

Overview

Because you're ruled by 6 this year, love is in the air! Venus, Taurus and Libra are well known for their affinity with romance, love, and even marriage. If ever you were going to meet a soulmate and feel comfortable in love, 2009 must surely be your year.

Taurus has a strong connection to money and practical affairs as well, so finances will also improve if you are diligent about work and security issues.

The important thing to keep in mind this year is that sharing love and making that important soul connection should be kept high on your agenda. This will be an enjoyable period in your life.

Love and pleasure

Romance is the key thing for you this year and your current relationships will become more fulfilling if you happen to be attached. For singles, a 6 year heralds an important meeting that eventually leads to marriage.

You'll also be interested in fashion, gifts, jewellery and all sorts of socialising. It's at one of these social engagements that you could meet the love of your life. Remain available!

Venus is one of the planets that has a tendency to overdo things, so be moderate in your eating and drinking. Try generally to maintain a modest lifestyle.

Work

You'll have a clearer insight into finances and your future security during a number 6 year. Whereas you may have had additional expenses and extra distractions previously, your mind will be more settled and capable of longer-term planning along these lines.

With the extra cash you might see this year, decorating your home or office will give you a special sort of satisfaction.

Social affairs and professional activities will be strongly linked. Any sort of work-related functions may offer you romantic opportunities as well. On the other hand, be careful not to mix up your workplace relationships with romantic ideals. This could complicate some of your professional activities.

Improving your luck

You'll want more money and a life of leisure and ease in 2009. Keep working on your strengths and eliminate your negative personality traits to create greater luck and harmony in your life.

Moderate all your actions and don't focus exclusively on money and material objects. Feed your spiritual needs as well. By balancing the inner and outer you'll see that your romantic and professional life will be enhanced more easily.

The 1st, 8th, 15th and 20th hours on Fridays will be very lucky for you and new opportunities will arise for you at those times. You can use the numbers 6, 15, 24 and 33 to increase luck in your general affairs.

7 = Year of Neptune

Overview

The last and most evolved sign of the zodiac is Pisces, which is ruled by Neptune. The number 7 is deeply connected with this zodiacal sign and governs you in 2009. Your ideals seem to be clearer and more spiritually orientated than ever before. Your desire to evolve and understand your inner self will be a double-edged sword. It depends on how organised you are as to how well you can use these spiritual and abstract concepts in your practical life.

Your past emotional hurts and deep emotional issues will be dealt with and removed for good, if you are serious about becoming a better human being.

Spend a little more time caring for yourself rather than others, as it's likely some of your friends will drain you of energy with their own personal problems. Of course, you mustn't turn a blind eye to the needs of others, but don't ignore your own personal needs in the process.

Love and pleasure

Meeting people with similar life views and spiritual aspirations will rekindle your faith in relationships. If you do choose to develop a new romance, make sure that there is a clear under-standing of the responsibilities of one to the other. Don't get swept off your feet by people who have ulterior motives.

Keep your relationships realistic and see that the most idealistic partnerships must eventually come down to Earth. Deal with the practicalities of life.

Work

This is a year of hard work, but one in which you'll come to understand the deeper significance of your professional ideals. You may discover a whole new aspect to your career, which involves a more compassionate and self-sacrificing side to your personality.

You'll also find that your way of working will change and that you'll be more focused and able to get into the spirit of whatever you do. Finding meaningful work is very likely and therefore this could be a year when money, security, creativity and spirituality overlap to bring you a great sense of personal satisfaction.

Tapping into your greater self through meditation and self-study will bring you great benefits throughout 2009.

Improving your luck

Using self-sacrifice along with discrimination will be an unusual method of improving your luck. The laws of karma state that what you give, you receive in greater measure. This is one of the principal themes for you in 2009.

The 1st, 8th, 15th and 20th hours of Tuesdays are your lucky times. The numbers 7, 16, 25 and 34 should be used to increase your lucky energies.

8 = Year of Saturn

Overview

The earthy and practical sign of Capricorn and its ruler Saturn are intimately linked to the number 8, which rules you in 2009. Your discipline and far-sightedness will help you achieve great things in the coming year. With cautious discernment, slowly but surely you will reach your goals.

It may be that due to the influence of the solitary Saturn, your best work and achievement will be behind closed doors away from the limelight. You mustn't fear this as you'll discover many new things about yourself. You'll learn just how strong you really are.

Love and pleasure

Work will overshadow your personal affairs in 2009, but you mustn't let this erode the personal relationships you have. Becoming a workaholic brings great material successes but will also cause you to become too insular and aloof. Your family members won't take too kindly to you working 100-hour weeks.

Responsibility is one of the key words for this number and you will therefore find yourself in a position of authority that leaves very little time for fun. Try to make time to enjoy the company of friends and family and by all means schedule time off on the weekends as it will give you the peace of mind you're looking for.

Because of your responsible attitude it will be very hard for you not to assume a greater role in your workplace and this indicates longer working hours with the likelihood of a promotion with equally good remuneration.

Work

Money is high on your agenda in 2009. Number 8 is a good money number according to the Chinese and this year is at last likely to bring you the fruits of your hard labour. You are cautious and resourceful in all your dealings and will not waste your hard-earned savings. You will also be very conscious of using your time wisely.

You will be given more responsibilities and you're likely to take them on, if only to prove to yourself that you can handle whatever life dishes up.

Expect a promotion in which you will play a leading role in your work. Your diligence and hard work will pay off, literally, in a bigger salary and more respect from others.

Improving your luck

Caution is one of the key characteristics of the number 8 and is linked to Capricorn. But being overly cautious could cause you to miss valuable opportunities. If an offer is put to you, try to think outside the square and balance it with your naturally cautious nature.

Be gentle and kind to yourself. By loving yourself, others will naturally love you, too. The 1st, 8th, 15th and 20th hours of Saturdays are exceptionally lucky for you as are the numbers 1, 8, 17, 26 and 35.

9 = Year of Mars

Overview

You are now entering the final year of a nine-year cycle dominated by the planet Mars and the sign of Aries. You'll be completing many things and are determined to be successful after several years of intense work.

Some of your relationships may now have reached their use-by date and even these personal affairs may need to be released. Don't let arguments and disagreements get in the road of friendly resolution in these areas of your life.

Mars is a challenging planet and, this year, although you will be very active and productive, you may find others trying to obstruct the achievement of your goals. As a result you may react strongly to them, thereby creating disharmony in your workplace. Don't be so impulsive or reckless, and generally slow things down. The slower, steadier approach has greater merit this year.

Love and pleasure

If you become too bossy and pushy with friends this year you will just end up pushing them out of your life. It's a year to end certain friendships but by the same token it could be the perfect time to end conflicts and thereby bolster your love affairs in 2009.

If you're feeling a little irritable and angry with those you love, try getting rid of these negative feelings through some intense, rigorous sports and physical activity. This will definitely relieve tension and improve your personal life.

Work

Because you're healthy and able to work at a more intense pace you'll achieve an incredible amount in the coming year. Overwork could become a problem if you're not careful.

Because the number 9 and Mars are infused with leadership energy, you'll be asked to take the reins of the job and steer your company or group in a certain direction. This will bring with it added responsibility but also a greater sense of purpose for you.

Improving your luck

Because of the hot and restless energy of the number 9, it is important to create more mental peace in your life this year. Lower the temperature, so to speak, and decompress your relationships rather than becoming aggravated. Try to talk to your work partners and loved ones rather than telling them what to do. This will generally pick up your health and your relationships.

The 1st, 8th, 15th and 20th hours of Tuesdays are the luckiest for you this year and, if you're involved in any disputes or need to attend to health issues, these times are also very good for the best results. Your lucky numbers are 9, 18, 27 and 36

2009:
Your Daily Planner

> *I cannot give you the formula for success, but I can give you the*
> *formula for failure—which is: Try to please everybody.*
>
> —Herbert Bayard Swope

There is a little-known branch of astrology called electional astrology, and it can help you select the most appropriate times for many of your day-to-day activities.

Ancient astrologers understood the planetary patterns and how they impacted on each of us. This allowed them to suggest the best possible times to start various important activities. Many farmers today still use this approach: they understand the phases of the Moon, and attest to the fact that planting seeds on certain lunar days produces a far better crop than planting on other days.

The following section covers many areas of daily life, and uses the cycles of the Moon and the combined strength of the other planets to work out the best times to start different types of activity.

So to create your own personal almanac, first select the activity you are interested in, and then quickly scan the year for the best months to start it. When you have selected the month, you can finetune your timing by finding the best specific dates. You can then be sure that the planetary energies will be in sync with you, offering you the best possible outcome.

Coupled with what you know about your monthly and weekly trends, the daily planner can be a powerful tool to help you capitalise on opportunities that come your way this year.

Good luck, and may the planets bless you with great success, fortune and happiness in 2009!

Starting activities

How many times have you made a new year's resolution to begin a diet or be a better person in your relationships? And how many times has it not worked out? Well, the reason may be partly that you started out at the wrong time! How successful you are is strongly influenced by the position of the Moon and the planets when you begin a particular activity. You could be more successful with the following activities if you start them on the days indicated.

Relationships

We all feel more empowered on some days than on others. This is because the planets have some power over us—their movement and their relationships to each other determine the ebb and flow of our energies. And our level of self-confidence and our sense of romantic magnetism play an important part in the way we behave in relationships.

Your daily planner tells you the ideal dates for meeting new friends, initiating a love affair, spending time with family and loved ones—it even tells you the most appropriate times for sexual encounters.

You'll be surprised at how much more impact you make in your relationships when you tune yourself in to the planetary energies on these special dates.

Falling in love/restoring love

During these times you could expect favourable energies to meet your soulmate or, if you've had difficulty in a relationship, to approach the one you love to rekindle both your and their emotional responses:

January	28, 30
February	25, 26
March	6, 7, 8, 28, 29, 30
April	25, 26, 30
May	1, 2, 5, 7, 26, 27, 28, 29

June	2, 3, 23, 24, 26, 29, 30
July	22, 23, 26, 27
August	14, 15, 16, 17, 22, 23, 24
September	10, 14, 16, 19, 20, 21
October	9, 10, 11, 12, 13
November	25, 26
December	22, 23, 27, 31

Special times with friends and family

Socialising, partying and having a good time with those you enjoy being with is highly favourable under the following dates. These dates are excellent to spend time with family and loved ones in a domestic environment:

January	26
February	8, 12, 13, 14, 22, 23, 24
March	8, 22, 23
April	19, 27, 28
May	1, 2, 15, 16, 17, 24, 25, 28, 29
June	2, 3, 11, 12, 13, 22, 30
July	23, 26, 27
August	5, 6, 23, 24
September	16
October	13
November	8, 10, 24
December	19, 20, 21, 29

Healing or resuming relationships

If you're trying to get back together with the one you love and need a heart-to-heart or deep and meaningful, you can try the following dates to do so:

January	5, 8, 11, 12, 18, 19, 20, 21, 22, 23, 24, 25, 26, 28, 30
February	8, 12, 13, 14
March	8
April	18, 19
May	1, 2, 28, 29
June	2, 3, 30
July	23, 26, 27
August	23, 24
September	16
October	13
November	8
December	22, 23, 27

Sexual encounters

Physical and sexual energies are well favoured on the following dates. The energies of the planets enhance your moments of intimacy during these times:

January	5, 30
February	25, 26
March	6, 7, 8, 28, 29, 30
April	25, 26, 30
May	1, 2, 5, 7, 26, 27, 28, 29

June	2, 3, 23, 24, 26, 29, 30
July	22, 23, 26, 27
August	23, 24
September	16
October	13
November	25, 26
December	22, 23, 27, 31

Health and wellbeing

Your aura and life force are susceptible to the movements of the planets; in particular, they respond to the phases of the Moon.

The following dates are the most appropriate times to begin a diet, have cosmetic surgery, or seek medical advice. They also tell you when the best times are to help others.

Feeling of wellbeing

Your physical as well as your mental alertness should be strong on these following dates. You can plan your activities and expect a good response from others:

January	8, 9, 26, 27
February	4, 5, 22, 23
March	31
April	18, 19, 27, 28
May	16, 17
June	21, 22
July	19
August	5, 6, 24, 25

September	12, 28, 30
October	8, 9
November	8, 10
December	19, 20, 21, 29, 30

Healing and medicine

This is good for approaching others who have expertise at a time when you need some deeper understanding. This is also favourable for any sort of healing or medication and making appointments with doctors or psychologists. Planning surgery around these dates should bring good results.

Often giving up our time and energy to assist others doesn't necessarily result in the expected outcome. By lending a helping hand to a friend on the following dates, the results should be favourable:

January	1, 20, 21, 22, 23, 24, 25, 26, 27, 28, 29, 30, 31
February	9, 10, 11, 12, 13, 14, 15, 16, 17, 18, 19, 20, 21, 22, 23, 24, 25, 26, 27, 28
March	2, 3, 4, 5, 6, 7, 8, 9, 22, 26, 28, 29, 30, 31
April	1, 10, 12, 15, 18, 20, 27, 28, 29, 30
May	1, 3, 7, 8, 9, 10, 11, 12
June	6, 7, 9, 13, 14, 15, 19, 21, 22
July	5, 6, 7, 8, 10, 12, 18, 19, 20, 25, 26
August	6, 7, 8, 9, 10, 29, 30, 31
September	1, 6, 27
October	8, 9, 10, 11, 12, 25, 26
November	18, 19, 20, 21, 22
December	10, 11, 12

Money

Money is an important part of life, and involves many decisions; decisions about borrowing, investing, spending. The ideal times for transactions are very much influenced by the planets, and whether your investment or nest egg grows or doesn't grow can often be linked to timing. Making your decisions on the following dates could give you a whole new perspective on your financial future.

Managing wealth and money

To build your nest egg, it's a good time to open your bank account and invest money on the following dates:

January	3, 4, 5, 10, 11, 16, 17, 23, 24, 25, 31
February	1, 6, 7, 12, 13, 14, 20, 21, 27, 28
March	5, 6, 7, 12, 13, 19, 26, 27
April	2, 3, 8, 9, 15, 17, 23, 24, 29, 30
May	5, 6, 7, 13, 14, 20, 21, 26, 27
June	2, 3, 9, 10, 16, 17, 18, 23, 24, 29, 30
July	6, 7, 8, 14, 15, 20, 21, 26, 27
August	2, 3, 4, 10, 11, 17, 18, 23, 24, 30, 31
September	6, 7, 13, 14, 19, 20, 26, 27
October	3, 4, 5, 10, 11, 16, 17, 18, 23, 24, 25, 31
November	1, 6, 7, 13, 14, 20, 21, 27, 28
December	4, 5, 10, 11, 17, 18, 24, 25, 26, 31

Spending

It's always fun to spend but the following dates are more in tune with this activity and are likely to give you better results:

January	20, 28, 30
February	3
March	28, 29, 30
April	25, 26
May	31
June	1, 2, 7, 8, 9, 10, 28, 30
July	1, 2, 3, 26, 27, 29, 30
August	2, 3, 4, 5, 20, 21, 22, 23, 24, 25
September	19, 20, 21, 22, 23
October	9, 10
November	1, 7, 8, 17
December	27, 28

Selling

If you're thinking of selling something, whether it is small or large, consider the following dates as ideal times to do so:

January	3, 18, 19, 20, 21, 25, 26, 27, 28, 29, 30, 31
February	8, 10, 11, 12, 13, 14, 15, 18, 20, 22, 23, 24, 26, 28
March	2, 3, 4, 5, 6, 7, 8, 9, 16, 26, 27, 28, 31
April	5, 10, 19, 20, 23, 25, 27, 28, 29
May	1, 2, 7, 9, 13, 14, 21, 24, 25, 28, 29, 31
June	1, 2, 7, 8, 14, 16, 17, 20, 21, 22, 26, 30
July	1, 2, 3, 9, 10, 11, 15, 16, 17, 26, 27
August	2, 3, 4, 13, 14, 15, 16, 17
September	1, 2, 3, 4, 5, 6, 14, 15, 16, 17, 21, 22, 23, 24, 25, 26, 27, 28, 30, 31

October	1, 2, 3, 4, 5, 6, 7, 8, 9, 10, 11, 12, 31
November	2, 3, 9, 10, 11, 12, 13, 25, 26, 27, 28, 29, 30
December	1, 2, 3, 7, 8, 9, 17, 20

Borrowing

Few of us like to borrow money, but if you must, taking out a loan on the following dates should be positive:

January	11, 18, 19, 20, 23, 24, 25
February	15, 16, 20, 21
March	14, 15, 19, 20
April	10, 11, 12, 15, 16, 17
May	9, 13, 14
June	9, 10
July	7, 8, 20, 21
August	17, 18
September	13, 14
October	10, 11
November	6, 7, 15, 16
December	4, 5, 12, 13, 14

Work and education

Your career is important to you, and continual improvement of your skills is therefore also crucial, professionally, mentally and socially. The dates below will help you find out the most appropriate times to improve your professional talents and commence new work or education associated with your work.

You may need to decide when to start learning a new skill, when to ask for a promotion, and even when to make an important career change. Here are the days when mental and educational power is strong.

Learning new skills

Educational pursuits are lucky and bring good results on the following dates:

January	8, 9
February	4, 5
March	3, 4, 10, 31
April	1, 6, 7, 27, 28
May	3, 4, 25, 30, 31
June	1, 6, 7, 27, 28
July	4, 5, 24, 25, 31
August	1, 21, 22, 27, 28, 29
September	23, 24, 25
October	21, 22
November	17, 18, 19
December	29, 30

Changing career path or profession

If you're feeling stuck and need to move into a new professional activity, changing jobs can be done at these times:

January	6, 7
February	2, 3
March	1, 2, 3, 4, 5, 6, 7, 8, 9, 10, 28, 29, 30
April	6, 7, 25, 26
May	3, 4, 30, 31
June	1, 27, 28

July	6, 24, 25
August	2, 3, 4, 21, 22, 30, 31
September	26, 27
October	23, 24, 25
November	2, 20, 21, 29, 30
December	1, 17, 18, 27, 28

Promotion, professional focus and hard work

To increase your mental focus and achieve good results from the work you do, promotions are likely on these dates that follow:

January	4, 5, 6, 11, 12, 13, 14, 15, 16, 21
February	6
March	18, 19, 20
April	8, 28, 29
May	12, 21
June	25, 26
July	1, 2, 3, 8, 15, 17
August	4, 14, 15, 16, 17, 18, 22, 23, 24
September	14, 15, 18, 19, 23, 24, 25, 26
October	22
November	7, 10, 11, 12, 17
December	1, 2, 3, 7, 28

Travel

Setting out on a holiday or adventurous journey is exciting. To
in the most out of your holidays and journeys, travelling on
following dates is likely to give you a sense of fulfilment:

January	9, 10, 28, 29, 30, 31
February	1, 4, 5, 26
March	3, 4, 5, 6, 7, 27, 31
April	27, 28, 29
May	1, 2, 25
June	6, 7, 25, 26
July	6, 31
August	1, 2, 21, 22, 23, 24, 29
September	19, 20, 23, 24, 25, 26, 27
October	1, 2, 3, 25, 28, 29, 30, 31
November	1, 17, 18, 26, 28
December	17, 18, 23, 26

Beauty and grooming

Believe it or not, cutting your hair or nails has a powerful effect on your body's electromagnetic energy. If you cut your hair or nails at the wrong time of the month, you can reduce your level of vitality significantly. Use these dates to ensure you optimise your energy levels by staying in tune with the stars.

Hair and nails

January	1, 2, 8, 9, 21, 22, 28, 29, 30
February	4, 5, 17, 18, 19, 25, 26
March	3, 4, 16, 17, 18, 24, 25, 31
April	1, 13, 14, 20, 21, 22, 27, 28, 29, 30
May	8, 10, 11, 12, 18, 19, 24, 25
June	6, 7, 8, 14, 15, 21, 22

July	4, 5, 11, 12, 13, 18, 19, 31
August	1, 7, 8, 9, 14, 15, 16, 27, 28, 29
September	4, 5, 11, 12, 23, 24, 25
October	1, 2, 8, 9, 21, 22, 28, 29, 30
November	4, 5, 17, 18, 19, 25, 26
December	2, 3, 15, 16, 22, 23, 29, 30

Therapies, massage and self-pampering

January	18, 19, 20, 26, 27
February	3, 6, 7, 8, 12, 13, 14, 15, 16, 22, 23, 24
March	6, 8, 28, 29, 30
April	5, 8, 9, 18, 19, 25, 26, 29, 30
May	1, 2, 5, 7, 9, 15, 16, 17, 22, 23, 26, 27, 28, 29
June	2, 3, 4, 5, 11, 12, 13, 19, 20, 23, 24, 26, 30
July	1, 2, 3, 9, 10, 23, 26, 27, 28, 29, 30
August	6, 12, 13, 17, 18, 19, 20, 23, 24, 25, 26
September	1, 2, 13, 14, 16
October	10, 11, 12, 13, 16, 17, 27
November	8, 9, 10, 13, 16, 23, 24, 29, 30
December	1, 4, 5, 6, 7, 10, 11, 12, 13, 14, 19, 20, 21, 27, 28, 31

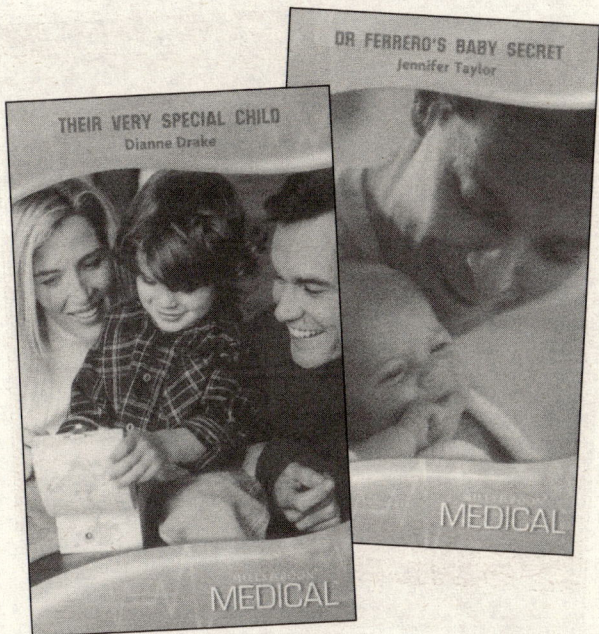

CHRÈSTINA x,
TARA
23. 05 (19